IMAGES
of England

AROUND
PENRYN

Kind Regards

Erie Warrington

At Bohelland (very near to St Gluvias' church, Penryn) a tragedy took place in the seventeenth century. The particulars of this dreadful affair were detailed in a pamphlet published in 1618 entitled: 'News from PERIN in Cornwall of a most bloody and unexampled murther very lately committed by a Father on his own sonne at the instigation of a mercilesse Step-Mother, being all performed in the month of September last, anno 1618'. This grim event was made into a thrilling play at the Haymarket and again at Drury Lane, London.

A younger son of a Penryn merchant went to sea and got into the hands of pirates. Coming ashore at Rhodes, he offered some jewels for sale. They were recognized by a Jew as belonging to the Governor of Algiers; being sentenced as a pirate he was sent to the galley. Cleverer than his fellow slaves, his courage found him aboard an English ship bound for England, where he became a servant to a surgeon and eventually sailed to the East Indies. He was away for fifteen years and came home with much gold and jewellery concealed on him.

Concealing his identity from his parents, he told his sister (who did not reside at home) about his exploits and swore her to secrecy. The old couple took him in and were enchanted by his tales. His mother wept at his stories and he comforted her with a piece of gold. The thought of his wealth was too much for them; they let him stay and during the night murdered him. His sister asked for the sailor that had lodged there for the night, but the old folk denied knowing him. She told them who he was and mentioned a scar on his arm. The father found the mark to be true and in remorse took his own life. The mother did the same and the daughter, overcome with grief and horror at the sight, died herself.

IMAGES
of England

AROUND
PENRYN

Compiled by
Ernie Warmington
with royalty proceeds going to
The Cancer Research Campaign

TEMPUS

First published 2000
Copyright © Ernie Warmington, 2000

Tempus Publishing Limited
The Mill, Brimscombe Port,
Stroud, Gloucestershire, GL5 2QG

ISBN 0 7524 2098 4

Typesetting and origination by
Tempus Publishing Limited
Printed in Great Britain by
Midway Clark Printing, Wiltshire

Foreword

It gives me great pleasure to write this foreword to the second book written for the Cancer Research Campaign by Ernie Warmington. The people of Cornwall have played a crucial role in raising money for vital research work. Great benefits are achieved every day, from the drugs, treatments, clinical trials and cures discovered by the Campaign. This research is funded entirely by voluntary contributions, and I wish Ernie every success with his second book.

Beverly Bell
Senior Fundraising Manager – Cornwall

Contents

Acknowledgements

However much you may think you know your home town, where you were born, where you lived, were schooled and were brought up, there is always someone whom you can turn to for more information. This book is really a continuation of my previous book on Penryn written two years ago for the Cancer Research Campaign. I had hundreds of postcards and photographs left over. I simply had to write another, again for Cancer Research, and there are still hundreds left. I am fortunate enough to know a lot a people in Penryn and have made many more friends in the villages I have newly covered, to whom I am deeply grateful. I would like to thank all the following people:

Cllr Mary May, Mayor of Penryn, for the loan of some photographs from the museum's archives, Eric Dawkins (Penryn's Town Clerk), Peter Gilson, Shirley Richards, Alan Wills, Graham Jacket, Carol James, my friend Mrs Florrie Miller, Wendy and Tony Toy, Gerald Collins, Ron Rashleigh, Keith Bryant, Raymond Thomas, Jo Gluyas, Jo Moore, Christine Smith, John Basher, Trevor Dungate, Mrs R. Hodges, the Revd Graham Warmington, Tony Kerslake, Kitty Kneebone, Mrs Champion, Eric Clarke, Mrs Perham, Ron Doney, Maureen Willey, John Tregonning, Rosemary and Roy Webber, Mary Arthur, Mrs Coad, Len Tresidder, Alan Cross, Roger Dobbell, Betty Jenkin, Mrs Mandle, Nick Berringer, Val Martin, Nessie and Michael Simcock, Sylvia King, Russell Webber, William Rickard, Robert Patterson, Tony Gosling, Brian Richards, Jimmy Driscoll, Roma Woods.

For any names I have missed out or spelt incorrectly, or any places or dates I have got wrong, I apologize. This book has been written with my knowledge of my home town and information received from newly found friends in the outlying villages. My thanks must go to everyone who helped me to compose the book, especially my wife Rosemary who typed the text and put up with a disrupted household for at least six months. Once again it is dedicated to my parents and brother Reggie, who died of cancer. The royalties of this book go once again to The Cancer Research Campaign.

Introduction

The picturesque and proud port of Penryn is situated in the south west of Cornwall at the head of the Penryn river which flows down into the Falmouth harbour, covers some 900 acres and has a population of approximately 6,000. Stretching over three sides of a wooded valley it is one of the most ancient boroughs in Cornwall; Treliver, a part of the town, is mentioned in the *Domesday Book* (see illustration further on in this book) and it has a wealth of character and charm and a port of some significance.

Penryn was founded as a town in 1216. It received its first charter for markets in 1236, and was sending two members to Parliament as early as 1547 (not 1553 as first thought). It received its first charter as a borough from James I in 1621 with Sampson Boyle as the first mayor. The great Collegiate Church of St Thomas, Glasney, was built in 1265 by Walter Bromscombe, Bishop of Exeter, as a result of a dream experienced during an illness, that instructed him to found a religious college on marshy land at Glasney. The church is documented in 1334. The Priory was completed in two years and built using local granite and labour as well as stone brought from Caen in Normandy. Constructed on a six-acre site, it was strongly defended against surprise attack by Spanish and French pirates with three fortified towers and a chain boom across the head of the creek. The college was later closed by Henry VIII at the Reformation. The church roof was stripped of its lead, which is believed to have been shipped to the Isles of Scilly. The rest of the buildings were sold, and much of the better and more finely worked pieces of stone were used for prominent buildings and homes locally. For example, a gargoyle can be seen projecting from a wall at the top of St Gluvias Street as well as other places throughout the town. There are quite a few shaped stones and carved relics to be seen in the town's museum. If the college had not been destroyed during the Reformation, without any doubt it would have been one of the leading schools not only in Cornwall but England, and Penryn would be a cathedral city instead of Truro, as we know it today.

As a port, there was little trade during the fourteenth century but in the following years the town grew to become one of the principal ports in the area. In the Tudor years and for quite some time afterwards it shared with other ports in the area the distinction of having more shipping than any other port in the country.

The development of Cornish tin and copper mining in the seventeenth century brought renewed prosperity to the town and the port handled many of the early tin exports from mines in the Camborne-Redruth area. Sir Peter Killigrew, being a businessman, saw the potential of this and with the help of Sir Walter Raleigh (returning home from the West Indies) managed to move the customs due from Penryn to the newly developing hamlet of Penny-Come-Quick. Penryn petitioned the King, but James I agreed to the building of the port at the new town of Falmouth. Falmouth was granted its first charter in 1661, making it 400 years younger than Penryn.

Falmouth developed very quickly and caused a serious decline in trade for Penryn for a great many years. However, the early nineteenth century produced an industry which was to be a factor in returning Penryn to the prosperity it had known centuries before. Large deposits of finest granite stone were being quarried in the little villages around the town, Mabe and Constantine in particular. The stone was brought to the works and quays alongside the river by horses and traction engines; thus Penryn became known as the Granite Port. From these famous quays and wharves dressed granite, a fine, durable, grey stone, was shipped from John Freeman's yard. It was used not only in some of London's notable public buildings, such as the Old Bailey and Lambeth and Putney Bridges, but also all over the world, as far afield as Gibraltar and Singapore. With the wider use of concrete in the twentieth century, there was once again a decline in Penryn's export trade, and Freeman's yard and works closed thirty-five years ago. However, many of the granite quarries still produce stone for facing large buildings and for road and house construction.

As the reader will see from the postcards and photographs, Penryn was once a thriving busy town, as were other Cornish towns and villages; they were almost entirely self-sufficient. Almost all kinds of tradesmen lived in the town – blacksmiths, wheelwrights, brewers, mill workers, rope makers – the list is endless. Shops were late in closing; even at Christmas time they stayed open until midnight. The streets thronged with people and light traffic, mostly horses and carts until the advent of the internal combustion engine in the early 1900s. Business owners and delivery men gradually changed over to little lorries and vans with people being able to go further afield than they did with their horse transport.

Around Penryn are also some delightful villages, many of which are also featured in this book.

FROM MAIOR TO MAIOR
TO THE TOWNE OF PERMARIN
WHEN THEY RECEIVED MEE THAT
WAS IN GREAT MISERY.

For over 360 years a ritual has been observed at the annual Mayor-making Ceremony, whereby the departing Mayor presents a huge silver Loving Cup to his/her successor. The story of this cup is a strange one. Many historians accuse Jane Killigrew of piracy, adultery and other crimes. Lady Jane was the daughter of Sir George Fermor of Northamptonshire and married at a young age. She took with her a dowry to Sir John Killigrew of Arwenack, the manor house near the harbour at Falmouth. It was not a happy marriage and in 1613 Lady Jane was accused of adultery with the Governor of Pendennis Castle, Sir Nicholas Parker, and she fled to Penryn. The Mayor and people had little love for the Killigrews and gave her refuge for the next twenty years. When Sir John died in 1633 Lady Jane returned to Arwenack. On her departure from Penryn she presented the famous cup to the Mayor and town 'for ever'. It has a capacity of 6 pints and was valued in 1633 at £12. It is now priceless and is Penryn's prize possession.

One

Early Days, Houses, Churches and Chapels

This print of 1831 shows the view towards Flushing, at that time a little fishing village, from halfway up Helston Road. St Gluvias' church is on the left together with the slate roofs of the houses of West Street, as we know it. At various points this street has been known as Pig Street, Calver Street and North Street. The cows may be on their way to the abattoir. The small thatched houses on the right were built and rented out by the Bassetts, a well-known Cornish family, for what would seem a little rent to us now. A few little ships can be seen coming up the river. The amount of trees and shrubs on the left is surprising: they are now gone and houses are in their place.

> **Terra Epi de Excecestre.**
>
> Epis Exoniensis tenet Treluuel T.R.E. geldb p.i. hida 7 dimid. Tra e. xx. car. In dnio fu. ii. car. 7 iiii. serui. 7 xxx. uilli 7 iiii. bord cu. xii. car. Ibi pastura. ii. leu lg. 7 ii. leu lat. 7 lx. ac siluæ. Olim 7 modo ual. iiii. lib.
>
> De eps ten Maæele T.R.E. geldb p.i. hida. sed tam ibi e una hida 7 dim. Tra. e. xx. car. In dnio. e. i. car. 7 iiii. serui. 7 xv. uilli 7 iiii. bord cu. vii. car. Ibi. xl. ac pasturæ. 7 lx. ac siluæ minutæ. Olim 7 modo ual. xl. solid.
>
> foru hui maneriu tc com mortton. qd eps habet T.R.E.

The earliest documented reference to Penryn is in the *Domesday Book*, the Great Survey of England ordered by William the Conqueror in 1086. It refers in detail to the manor of Treliwel (Treliver) held at that time by the Bishop of Exeter. The translation of the original Latin reads: 'Bishop of Exeter's Land in Cornwall. The Bishop has one manor which is called Treliwel which Bishop Leuric held T.R.E. and it rendered geld for $1\frac{1}{2}$ hides. Twenty teams can plough this. Thereof the Bishop has in demesne half a hide and the villeins have one hide and twelve ploughs. There the Bishop has thirty villeins and four boarders and four serfs and five unbroken mares and two cows and thirty sheep and sixty acres of woodland and of pasture two leagues in length and two in breadth. Then and now this manor is worth four Lib [pounds].'

The insignia of the borough of Penryn. A tremendous amount has been said, written and argued by historians for many a year (and will no doubt continue) about the origin of Penryn's insignia, the 'Saracen's Head'. The various descriptions are too numerous to give here, but the image basically consists of a bearded head with a laurel wreath and almost invariably looking to his left. It has been in use for hundreds of years and with a little luck will always be used. 'BVRGVS' is a Latin words for Burgesses, or Town.

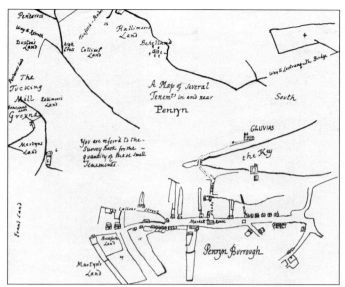

This very early map of Penryn and district is an interesting document. One notable feature is that some street names are different to those of today. To the right of the market house (along the top of the market house on the map) is Shute Lane, now known as St Gluvias Street. Today's Shute Lane is now to the left, nearly at the end of West Street. What the map names as Calver Street was later known as Pig Street and North Street. Gluvias church is shown, but was later rebuilt in the same style (in 1883) and is now known as St Gluvias church. There is believed to be a tunnel leading from the quay to the church or vicarage. As a youngster, with mates, I went a short distance up the tunnel to find it blocked off; when the candle was blown out it frightened the life out of us! This tunnel could well be a relic of the smuggling which must have gone on in Penryn centuries ago; the illicit trade in alcohol and tobacco is also remembered in *A Smuggler's Song* by Rudyard Kipling: 'Brandy for the Parson and baccy for the Clerk, so watch the wall my darling as the gentlemen go by'.

This engraved picture by an unknown artist of the south view of Penryn was drawn long before any motorized transport was invented. It seems that the driver of the horse and cart on the left is talking to the gentleman sitting on the wall – perhaps about the weather or an evening's 'disco' at the Temperance Hall! With the church on the right, the clock tower in the distance and the little ships tied up alongside, not a lot seems to be happening apart from the rowing boat heading for home: all looks peaceful and quiet.

A view from Mabe, above the busy towns of Penryn and Falmouth, *c.* 1850. In the background are the St Mawes and Falmouth Castles guarding the entrance to the bay and rivers. To the right of St Mawes Castle (on the left) is St Anthony lighthouse. Falmouth seems to be growing, with new developments of houses along the road at Greenbank. Piers, landing stages and large buildings are ready to accommodate the cargo about to be unloaded from the little ships in the harbour. In the foreground to the left is the town of Penryn with the church and clock tower visible, together with the houses in the main streets. Flushing (centre, on the left) looks nice and peaceful.

About $1\frac{1}{2}$ miles to the north of Penryn lies a handsome, silver-grey granite building, called Enys House. It is the home of the Enys family, who have owned it since the time of Edward I. It was originally built in the shape of an 'E' and is famed for its lovely gardens and fresh water lake. This delightful property was rebuilt by Samuel Enys who was a heavy gambler, reputed to have lost more than he had won. His oldest son John was Sheriff of Cornwall in 1751 and died in 1802. The property then passed on to his second son Francis. During the Second World War the Dutch Navy had their headquarters there.

Carclew House was bought in 1749 by William Lemon, a Truro mine owner and merchant, from James Bonython. His grandson, who later became Sir William Lemon, inherited the estate in 1760, passing it to Sir Charles, his second son, in 1824. Colonel Arthur Tremayne, Sir Charles' nephew, next owned it in 1868 who was in turn succeeded by his son Capt. Will Tremayne in 1905.

The head gardener (by the name of Luscombe) looked after the garden and estate at Carclew. Sir Charles Lemon grew a wonderful selection of rhododendron bushes and the estate was full of deer. From the picture, it would appear that the fountain was gravity-fed, as it seems to have quite a head, rising higher than the greenhouses. The palm trees could be 'dracaenas'. A fire mysteriously broke out in the early hours of 5 April 1934. Captain Tremayne's family and guests escaped in their night attire and were forced to watch the house be razed to the ground. Firemen attended from Truro, Penryn and Falmouth after being alerted by the family chauffeur who had to drive to the nearest station because it was found the telephone lines had been destroyed in the fire. The land and estate were sold for farming and housing.

A mile or so west of Penryn is a beautiful Georgian mansion, Tremough. Standing in its own grounds, it dates from Norman times and lies in the manor of Treliever. Treliever, of course, was mentioned in the *Domesday Book* of 1086. The land passed through several hands, including John Worth, who later became Sheriff of Cornwall. It was Worth who in 1703 built the mansion and stocked the grounds with deer. In July 1919, when the house was owned by Colonel Faulkner-Brown, the stables and clock tower were destroyed by fire. It has been suggested that the damage was so bad because firemen could not obtain any horses to pull the fire engine, which therefore had to be man-handled from the fire station and arrived too late.

The Convent of Notre Dame at Penryn, c. 1843. The convent was founded when three Catholics from Belgium came to Penryn to start a boarding school for local Catholics and a day school for the poor children of the town. From Mrs Edger, a recent convert to Catholicism, they bought the largest house in the main street at a reasonable price because it was haunted. This was a four-storey building, the foundations of which were said to be an old convent, made of local granite. It had a flat roof with a balustrade and a panoramic view over both town and river. It had three fruit gardens and a fountain, two sea-water swimming pools, stables and a coach house that led to a creek road at the bottom. In 1845 five Belgian Sisters were sent to Penryn to design the boarding school prospectus. There were threats from local Protestants when the school opened in 1846. The poor school prospered and pupil numbers rose to eighty by December. Two storeys were later added to the coach house, but further funds and buildings were sought without luck. By now the boarding school was struggling to survive. Sixty girls also attended lace-making and knitting classes, followed by religious instruction and prayers.

Below opposite: This lovely granite-built lodge house (no doubt made from local stone) stands at the entrance to the Tremough estate. While visiting India, Norman Gill, a nurseryman from Penryn, brought back some seeds of giant red, white and pink Himalayan rhododendrons which grew and are still flourishing in the grounds of the estate, a beautiful and wonderful setting for the Festival of Britain Pageant in 1951. The house then became a Roman Catholic Convent School but unfortunately was forced to close in 1999. There is now talk of the house and grounds, recently bought for the School of Arts, becoming the new University of Cornwall.

15

The poor school now numbered eighty-four, plus fifty-five girls in the Sunday school and thirteen boarders, which was remarkable given the opposition from the Methodists. Two Catholic men stood guard at Sunday school to reassure parents that the Sisters were not wicked and dangerous. It was said that children made the sign of the cross at the tollgate to get a free pass for Sunday worship. Because of local animosity, it was not until 1848 that Sisters were able to wear their habit whilst taking them for walks. The Sisters survived on charity alone, and because of the damp house, frequently became ill. One Sister, Maria Lane from Falmouth, died there and was buried in the garden. The community was at a low ebb in 1848 in view of the constant struggle and few converts, and the Sisters were recalled to Clapham. A week after most of the nuns left by packet boat for London, the last Mass was celebrated at Penryn. Mother Superior Claire and Sister Marie Alix went to Exeter by coach then by train to Clapham, arriving on 19 September 1848.

Penryn's parish church of St Gluvias. Built using local granite and labour, the church was consecrated by the Bishop of Exeter, Walter de Stapledon, in 1318. It was built on earlier foundations which could date back as far as the sixth century. While John Sheepshanks was vicar (1824-1845) the 'Church Plate Robbery' took place. On 5 October 1827 the sexton, John Tucker, found that the church had been broken into and the sacramental plate, bottles of wine and £1 12s 9d in cash had been taken and the poor box broken open. A reward of twenty guineas was offered after which three men were put into custody and charged with robbery, but the plate etc. was never found. As a new set was too expensive it was decided to purchase second-hand replacements. In September 1828 a silver flagon, chalice, paten and two plates costing £41 9s were bought by the churchwardens. On each article the following text was engraved: 'Parish of St Gluvias and Borough of Penryn by Voluntary Subscription 1828'. In 1883 the body of the church was restored in the style of the fifteenth century. The picture shows a carriage and pair, perhaps attending a wedding, being watched by someone in the doorway – but is that a ghost alongside the driver?

Something had to be done about the bells of St Gluvias church after the Second World War. It was found that because of the ravages of time and the effects of death-watch beetle they were potentially dangerous to ring. Generous donations by two families and money from another parishioner for a new frame meant the peal could be augmented to eight. Taylors of Loughborough removed the canons (bell fixings) and returned them with two newly cast trebles. Seen here are Charles Basher (left) with Cecil Richards in 1948 after the bells' removal.

Dedication of the bells at St Gluvias church. The Bishop of Truro, Dr J.W. Hankin, and the vicar, Canon Simcock, officiated with visiting clergy. The churchwardens, Cecil Richards, Charles Basher and the choir were also present at the dedication service for the augmented ring of eight bells on 19 March 1949.

This impressive old church at Constantine stands in a wonderful position high above a creek on the Helford River with magnificent rural views. Several churches have been built on this site; the previous one was Norman, and before that there was a Celtic church. Some stones remain from the Norman building. The present church was built in the fifteenth century from an immense supply of granite stone quarried locally. The chancel was built in 1862, all with local labour. The new steps in the churchyard had only just been completed when this picture was taken in 1858. Alongside them stands a new slate headstone dated 1857. A new slate roof was completed in 1879. What is surprising is the way the windows open up and down – or is there a large pane of glass missing?

Treluswell is a small village a short distance from Penryn on the Redruth Road, but big enough to attract this gathering of youngsters and older people. They are outside the Methodist chapel in 1935, dressed in their Sunday best; perhaps they are getting ready for their annual outing. Like so many others, the chapel it is now closed and the building is used by a local builder for storage.

MYLOR CHURCH PORCH & OLD CORNISH CROSS

This beautifully built church may date from as early as the twelfth century, but the Caen stone from which it is made could place it at a later date. As it was not usual to build in Cornwall with this imported stone shipped from French quarries, there is a very strong hint that the stone came from the Glasney Collegiate church when it was dismantled by Henry VIII. It took nine years, from 1870 to 1879, to restore the church, but in the process a lot of damage was caused, including the removal of the oak wagon roof of the late fourteenth century. The sandstone paving was taken up and even the thirteenth-century crucifix was placed outside, to decay from wind and rain. Seen here is the south porch, carved out of Caen stone with elaborately carved jambs; to the right is a tall, narrow stained-glass window and a majestic Cornish granite cross, typical of the county. This cross was found helping to support an unsafe wall, and when it was recovered it was found to be an exceptionally fine round-headed cross about 18ft long. Unfortunately its beauty is lost in the ground where it now stands, outside the door of Mylor church.

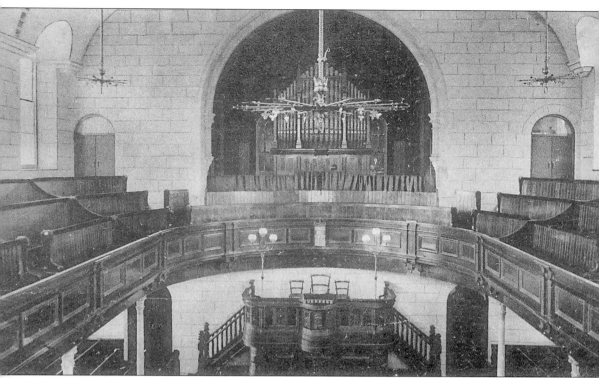

The interior of the Wesleyan chapel in the main street of Penryn. The first Methodist chapel was built in Chapel Lane in 1789 and was quite small. Because of a growing congregation the chapel was extended several times until 1848, when it had reached its capacity. The architect J.W. Trounson was appointed to oversee the construction of a new place of worship. Services were held in conjunction with the new church, conducted by the Revd E. Watson. On Whit Sunday, 18 May 1891, the memorial stones of the new school were laid. The proceedings were somewhat marred by rain during the ceremony. At 3 p.m. two memorial stones were laid by Miss Barrett, the senior teacher, on behalf of the school, and by Miss Silcox. The stones are on each side of the entrance. The sum of £25 was laid on each stone, and then twenty-four children followed, each laying a guinea on the stone. The chapel was built by Carkeeks of Redruth using local granite from John Freeman, at a cost of £5,000. It was opened on St Valentine's Day 1893. Dr Rigg conducted the last service in the old chapel in the morning and took the first service in the new chapel in the afternoon. The mayor, J.M. Thomas, conducted a band that had supported the choir. Curtis the local builder did the maintenance on the building at one time, and I can remember seeing Jack Truran the mason taking off the granite ball on the apex of the roof and standing in the cup, some 60 or 70ft from ground level.

The south side of Budock church, 1905. It was apparently almost entirely rebuilt in 1500. In that year Thomas Killigrew, a member of the famous Falmouth family (although hated in Penryn!) gave 1,500 marks (£1,000) towards the rebuilding. It is possible that any Norman work which then existed was removed and reused elsewhere. A.C.N. Vawdrey was vicar in 1908, the organist John Corder, organ blower Tom Truan and the cleaner was Mrs C. Rickard.

It is harvest festival time at the Bible Christian Chapel, West Street, with all the local produce of fruit and vegetables on display behind the people in the foreground. The chapel for 600 people was built in 1866 from local granite from the West Street (or Pig Street in those days) quarry. John Treneer was class leader and trustee of the chapel. With a dwindling congregation the members joined the Wesleyan folk further down The Terrace in November 1979. After being closed for quite some time, the chapel has now been converted into flats.

A poster for a concert of hymns at the United Methodist Church, *c.* 1949. According to the local paper of the time, it was very well attended. There was no admission charge and a programme cost only 6d; but in this way a reasonable amount of money was added to the choir and Sunday school funds. The poster was printed by Tommy Martin at his works in Commercial Road.

Members of the Carlidnack chapel, Mawnan Smith, *c.* 1950. The occasion was the sixtieth anniversary of the Sunday school. Mr C.B. Tallack, who lived nearby in a tiny cottage, was the genteel superintendent for many years. The building was later converted into a pleasant residence. From left to right, back row: Charles and Mrs Tallack, E. Ferris, C. Penrose, B. Musto, ? Pascoe, ? Chinn, ? Tresidder, ? Ould, ? Ferris. Second row: A. Tallack, C. Musto, L. Moore, -?-, G. Peppin, R. Forward, D. Harris, K. Jenkin. Front row: M. Christophers, J. Peppin, S. Christophers, -?-, M. Cocking, K. Peppin, -?-, -?-, M. Woodgate, -?-, C. Bailey.

Mawnan Smith United Methodist church tea treat, 1913. Participants are marching past the thatched cottage following the local band. No doubt the children were all excited on the day, looking forward to a lovely day of sports, a large saffron bun and a bottle of pop.

Mawnan Smith Band of Hope in the school playground, c. 1915. The back row includes Edwin Webster, Charles Row and Georgina Blee. On the front row are Laura and Arthur Webster, C. Rowe, Charles Tallack, -?-, -?-, ? Chiffers.

Two
Streets and Shops

Ponsanooth village, c. 1900. The third and present Methodist chapel is very prominent to the left of centre. The architect John Trevena was a local carpenter. The foundation stone was laid in March 1843 by William Jewell and the official opening took place in November. There was originally no heating and candles were the only form of lighting. The granite used came from local quarries, costing £1,300 – a rather high price, given that other chapels built within a few miles cost a great deal less. It seated over 600 people, including in the gallery. The Church incurred a large debt as a result of the construction, and by 1860 the debt was still £1,050. (This was at a time when farm labourers' wages were typically 2s a day.)

Longdowns, a hamlet near Mabe and four miles from Penryn on the Helston Road, *c.* 1900. Today's rules of the road were not enforced in this view: both vehicles are on the wrong side of the road! There were quarries in this area that provided Freeman's Granite Works with stone.

At the West End in Penryn this triumphal archway of foliage, flowers and bunting was erected to celebrate the Diamond Jubilee of Queen Victoria in 1897. She died four years later. The banner across both roads reads: 1837 GOD SAVE THE QUEEN 1897.

Brimicombe's shop (right) at the top of New Street, Penryn, c. 1900. The gentleman with the beard and silk top hat stands on the corner of St Thomas Street, to his right.

During the Reformation, King Henry VIII ordered the destruction of all monastic houses. Around Penryn some of the granite stones from the disused buildings were used to construct the Market House. This later became the Town Hall and had the Town Clock added. A little horse and cart slowly makes its way up Market Street in this scene from around 1900.

The bottom end of the main street at Mylor Bridge, c. 1905. On the right is the blacksmith's forge with a thatched roof; it was run by either David or William Reese. It is believed one of the first blacksmiths in the 17th century was a William Oak. They produced dredges, among other things, which were used by local oyster men plying their trade out on the oyster beds. Even today one of the little cottages is called The Forge. The lady on the left in the long fur-collared coat is taking her dog for a walk, while the little girl in the centre seems to have a high chair on wheels.

This is believed to be the water cart that came around the Mawnan Smith area before there was a mains supply. It dispensed water to households at a penny a bucket. The thatched cottage in the background has since been demolished.

Ponsanooth.

A view of Ponsanooth in 1905, from the Redruth end of the village. The photographer is standing on the bridge where young boys would fish for small trout in the fast flowing river Kennal. Two horses and carts are the only form of transport visible at a time when motor transport had yet to become common. The Stag Hunt inn is just around the corner on the left.

The bottom of St Peter's Terrace, Flushing, in 1905. The Standard Hotel is on the right with a gathering of locals interested in the photographer's activities. The houses on the right beyond the hotel were homes of some eminent local people in the shipping industry. For example, no. 8, a couple of doors past the leaning monkey-puzzle tree, housed Captain Bull. A right turn at the bottom of the hill leads to the Quays.

The Praze, Penryn, *c*. 1900. The houses on the right have since been demolished to make room for industrial development. Horse-drawn mail coaches used to go up the hill to the right towards Enys estate, then on to Carclew before their first change of horses at the Norway Inn.

The Cross Keys pub at The Praze, Penryn, *c*. 1900. The bicycle leaning against the wall is one of the then new 'safety' bicycles, to be distinguished from the more traditional 'ordinary' style, which we know as a penny-farthing. This establishment was owned in 1905 by Charlotte Ann Edwards, reputed to be a very hard landlady. The building looks as if it needs a lick of paint!

Penryn's main street, *c.* 1900. On the right is Mr Thomas's barber shop; in common with most barbers at the time he offered shaving as well, and also let some rooms. Money was raised by public subscription to light the four faces of the clock in memory of G.A. Jenkin, who had been Town Clerk of the borough for forty-eight years.

A prominent view of the black-faced town clock and Town Hall, which divides the street in two. On the right (in the shadow) are the largely residential properties of The Terrace. This area has undergone several periods of demolition, firstly to build the Wesleyan Chapel in 1893 and again in 1954 to make a road and build Saracen council housing estate.

An election rally at the top end of the village of Mylor, probably during the 1910 General Election campaign. Although the speaker has attracted the attention of the crowd, the soldiers in the car in front appear not to be interested! Note the Union Flag flying from the front car, and its prominent lamps, probably lit by acetylene. This vehicle could be a Humber, one of dozens of British makes of car which have since disappeared.

Fore Street, Constantine, *c.* 1900. It looks as if half the population have turned out for the photographer. Although the dog stood for the duration of the exposure, unfortunately some of the children on the left did not.

A general view of Ponsanooth, *c.* 1912. A small stream flows through this pretty village, which at one time supplied power to several mills, including a large woollen factory, flour mills and, most importantly, a gunpowder factory. The message on the reverse of the postcard says that the lady arrived at Penryn station 85 minutes late due to fog, and that as no car was available, she had to walk to Ponsanooth on Christmas Eve!

St Peter's Terrace, Flushing, 1906. This was once called New Road. On the left is St Peter's church, which was built in 1842 so the villagers did not have to walk to Mylor to worship. The building was funded by a benefactor, a Navy officer and packet captain, Adoniah Schnyler.

The Red Lion Inn, at the square in Mawnan Smith, during the Edwardian period. Not far from here are the delightful gardens of Glendurgan and Trebah created by the influential Quaker family, the Foxes.

The Terrace in Penryn in 1905. Some years later, the houses next to the shop on the right were demolished to make a new entrance to the Council School.

The junction of West Street and Helston Road, Penryn, 1905. The prominent house on the junction was known locally as the Lighthouse. West Street has had various other names through the years, including Pig Street and Calver Street.

Mylor village, just a few miles from Penryn, c. 1910. The horse and cart stands outside Bert Eskett-Williams Ash View Supply Store in the centre of the village. A little way down on the right is the Lemon Arms and further down on the left is the Tremayne Hall – both centres of activity in village life.

Constantine in around 1900, with the Cornish Arms Hotel on the right. The delightful granite cottages, no doubt built from locally quarried stone, are on Fore Street. The pub has since been renamed the Queen's Arms.

Near the stream in the village of Budock, c. 1905. It was here in February 1865 that, while ploughing a field, two local farm labourers named Tripp and Tallack found 1,000 Roman coins, surrounded by some sort of black material which crumbled in their hands. They were all examined by Dr T. Hodgkin, who decided they were buried in AD 306, early in the reign of Emperor Constantine, as part of a military chest belonging to a Roman officer. This serves to prove that the Romans had a significant presence in Cornwall at that time.

Ponsanooth village from outside the Stag Hunt inn. The road sweeps round to the right, over a little fast-flowing stream and onwards towards Redruth. The village lies on the borders of three parishes and at the centre of a group of little hamlets, including Laity Moor, Burnthouse, Pelean Cross and Kennal Vale. In 1841 there were 135 people living at Pelean Cross and Burnthouse.

Fish Cross, the original mouth of the Kersey stream at Flushing, in 1907. Crocker's grocery shop is behind the group of people, including the postman, children and fisherman. The road turning to the right is Kersey Road.

Broad Street, Penryn, in 1908. The horse-drawn bus stands outside Chapman's Hotel, which was later to become the King's Arms. On the extreme right is the purpose-built fire station with the stepped gable end and crossed axes between the windows; it was built in 1899.

Penryn's main street in 1910. The trees that were planted in 1902 to celebrate the Coronation of Edward VII are in full leaf. The little hut beneath the trees is believed to have provided shelter for the carriage drivers.

Here in Mawnan Smith motorized transport in the shape of a small bus (destination Falmouth) has taken over from the horse and cart. The lady and child may have just alighted from it. A local story has it that during the French wars the ladies of the village hurried down a narrow lane with pitchforks in hand and repelled an invasion from a French ship. The French saw their red petticoats and thought they were Redcoats approaching and retreated. The men of the village were very proud of them and called the lane 'Fire and Brave'.

St Gluvias Street, Penryn, still with cobbled pavements in around 1910. The fields in the background are now houses. The mail coaches may have gone down this route on their way to Truro, turning left at the bottom of the hill, although the post office was on The Terrace in 1853.

Market Street, Penryn, *c*. 1910. The cab on the right is waiting to be hired, and stands outside the Wesleyan Chapel, with two lanterns on the gate posts.

Wheal Vivian Stack at Constantine, *c*. 1910. The chimney was named after the landowner, Sir Richard Vivian, and this mine was the largest in the district. For this hard and dangerous work, the tin miner in the 1850s would earn £3 a month and bal-maidens (women employed at the tin mines on the surface breaking the stones) just £1. There were also mines at nearby Wheal Caroline which opened in 1850, and silver and lead deposits were mined at Wheal Anna Maria.

Down Top Street or Fish Cross, *c.* 1905. The latter name derives from the fact that some time before, women sold fish and oysters there. The view from the crossroads is towards the Market House and Town Clock. The horse-drawn mail van is being driven by Henry Penlerick.

A view over Penryn, the river and the railway viaduct from Kerwick Road.

Trefusis Street, Flushing, in 1928. The level of both this road and Coventry Street was raised in 1950 when mains water was brought to the village, and also to prevent the floods that sometimes occurred on spring tides. On the right is Pryor's grocers shop selling both Fry's and Cadbury's cocoa and chocolate.

Quay Hill, Penryn, c. 1935. Off to the left is the bridge and the road to Falmouth, where the lorry is possibly heading. Behind are the derelict offices of Cox & Sons, once a well-known hardware merchant and oil supplier in the town. On the extreme left is the old Anchor Hotel, now demolished.

The heavy snows of the winter of 1947 brought transport difficulties. This horse-drawn sledge laden with milk churns is at the top of Station Road, Penryn. This was once a private road owned by the GWR until it was bought by the council.

The New Quay at Flushing in 1930. The quay was built at Pencarven Point to protect the long waterfront from easterly gales. Where the photographer is standing the road turns sharply and leads to Trefusis Point. Half-way along this road there was once a silver and lead mine which extended under the sea. However, it only lasted for four years (1854-1858) as its proximity to the sea bed made it prone to flooding. After a particularly severe flood it was deemed dangerous and had to close. Unfortunately nothing now remains of the buildings or the mine.

Winter 1947 brought snow several feet thick which stayed for a number of weeks. The man is trudging his way up Helston Road, Penryn, with the town clock behind him.

Penryn's clock tower in the 1940s. The hackney carriage stand is outside the Methodist chapel. The photographer could have been standing near Pollard's butchers shop. Traffic calming and yellow lines had yet to arrive in the town.

A grocer's shop at 88 West Street, Penryn, at the turn of the twentieth century – the establishment belonged to the author's great-grandparents. The lady in the doorway could be the author's great-grandmother, Elizabeth. The man may not be her husband, John Edward, as he is wearing outdoor boots rather than the customary grocer's white apron. John died in 1899.

Fred Chegwidden worked for John Gill, a printer in Penryn who started a weekly free newspaper, *The Commercial Shipping and General Advertiser* in 1867. Fred looked after John when the latter retired and until his death in 1905 aged ninety-five. Fred and his wife Caroline (seen in the shop doorway) took over the shop near Fish Cross in 1898. The picture shows the picture postcards that were on sale, as well the *Western Mercury* newspaper; there was also a lending library.

Basher's grocers shop in The Praze, Penryn, *c.* 1915. Olive Basher is standing in the doorway and young Miss Basher and friend with their doll's pram are sitting on the doorstep. The young lad on the right could have been the errand boy. What a lovely window display, with hardly an inch to spare!

W.J. Tregoning was a market gardener and an expert flower grower who specialized in chrysanthemums and lived at Broad Street, Penryn. Here is a fine display of what he grew.

Fish Cross at the top of St Thomas Street. Jewell's grocery and fruit shop is on the corner, with Mrs Jewell in the doorway. There is a wide range of chocolate and cocoa on sale here. Penryn's fire station stood opposite, behind the photographer.

John Edward Warmington's grocers shop at the end of West Street, Penryn, opposite Mutton Row, c. 1920. The people gathered outside are wearing typical 1920s clothes. From left to right they are: Bessie Dawe, Annie Newcombe, William Charles Warmington (son of John Edward, who lived in the USA), his daughter Elizabeth, Belle Burrows.

Crocker's grocers shop at Flushing was established in 1886. Mrs Crocker is seen here in the doorway holding the baby. The windows carry the common Cadbury's Cocoa advertisements. The headline on the billboard reads 'The Terms of Surrender' – this probably dates the picture to the end of the Boer War in 1902. The small shop was modernised several times over the next few years and was finally demolished in the mid-1950s.

This is Edith and Jennie Thomas's grocers shop at Commercial Hill, Ponsanooth, in around 1920. The shop was built by their brother Oscar. The man standing on the left of the doorway with Edith is believed to be a Mr Dunstan. Jennie Thomas was reputed to be the house maid. Judging by the advertisements, they sold just about everything from beer to starch.

Mr Treloar standing proudly outside his photographic shop in Lower Market Street, Penryn, *c*. 1925. He also produced postcards. Some years before, the premises had been the Old Golden Lion pub.

This picture from around 1950 shows children playing near the Helford river. In 1825 a smuggler named Spry was caught lighting a fire to warn fellow smugglers of the approach of customs officers. He was apprehended and at his trial produced a testimonial to his good character from several respectable people, but to no avail – he was found guilty.

Trefusis Wood, Flushing, *c.* 1900. This was, and still is, a popular spot for families having a picnic and for schoolchildren's games, especially during school holidays. The beauty of the area was such that artists and painters would frequently be seen here.

Lower Street (later renamed Fore Street), Constantine, *c.* 1909. It seems that everything has come to a standstill to have this picture taken. Amongst the people on the right are Jack Medlyn who was a butcher and Arthur Jose (wearing an apron). The building on the right in the background was the Methodist chapel and is now in the process of being converted into a community centre.

A thatched cottage in Church Square, Constantine, *c.* 1909. At this time it was a butcher's shop owned by Mr Medlyn. The girl standing near the doorway dressed in white is Enid Rashleigh. Since this picture was taken the thatched roof has been removed and another storey has been added; the bottom is now renamed Rashleigh Court.

Fish Cross, Trefusis Street, Flushing, *c.* 1910. On the left is the old Sunset lodging house, and in front of this, at the left of the crowd, is Edwin Arthur, a coal merchant who was over seven feet tall. He used to escort ladies home after dark. On one occasion, while walking to Mylor and using a short cut, he fell into an open grave in the cemetery. As he climbed out, he frightened some revellers, who thought he was the Devil. He shouted after them, 'Be not afraid, 'tis only I.'

Trefusis Street, Flushing, *c.* 1915. The enamelled signs on the shop wall on the right are still recognizable from the previous picture, but where the old lodging house was on the left is now the new Seven Stars pub. It was on this site in 1810 that the mutiny of Post Office packet crew took place. Fishermen used to lay their fish for sale along the quay wall to the right of the picture.

With their purses and plates at the ready, Doris King and Winifred Badger are waiting for their meat ration from Mr Stevens, the butcher from Constantine, in Durgan, *c.* 1949. Margaret Badger is in the foreground by the chain-fence.

Three
Trains and Transport

The branch line from Truro to Falmouth opened in 1863. On 21 August a decorated train drawing thirteen carriages was greeted by the Mayor of Penryn and a large crowd at 12.47 p.m. The train reached Falmouth shortly after 1 p.m. There were 300 guests invited to a banquet in the evening, but no one from Penryn – including the Mayor – was officially invited. This is the original timber viaduct, with a panoramic view over the College Woods and Penryn in around 1890. Flushing is off to the left and the younger town of Falmouth is beyond. On the extreme left is the town clock showing two black faces. At the head of the river can just be seen the chimneys of Meads paper mill and Fox Stanton the timber merchant.

On Friday 31 October 1898 at 5.20 p.m. a mail train with passenger carriages was approaching Penryn. While travelling at a speed of 30 or 40mph it left the track on a bend and fell down a steep embankment, only coming to rest when the funnel became embedded in the slope. A cattle dealer by the name of Coombe rescued the driver, Cotterill, who was taken with the fireman Davey by cab to Truro. The driver died some time later from shock. Most of the thirty-three passengers were not injured and a relief train was sent for them from Truro. The picture shows the engine on its back, with its 5ft driving wheels in the air; the mail van is still attached.

On behalf of the Board of Trade, Colonel Yorke made a prolonged inspection together with a large number of Great Western Railway officials. Huge cranes were used to recover the train. The mail van was recovered in one piece but the engine had to be removed in pieces. A Penryn fire brigade member was called out from a warm bed, and subsequently caught pneumonia and died. Two gentlemen passengers who were wearing top hats emerged from a carriage with their headgear like concertinas.

Ponsanooth's old wooden viaduct over the valley was renewed in 1930, approximately four years before Penryn's College railway bridge was started. In this view the stone piers have been built and the wooden archways are in place on two of them, waiting for the masons to complete their work. The right-hand arch still has its steel supports and the carpenters are still working. At this point the old bridge is still in operation.

This was the last of Isambard Kingdom Brunel's timber viaducts to be completed on the Truro to Falmouth branch line, built in the mid-1860s. This magnificent wooden structure using a fan design over granite piers had fifteen spans, with a total length of 964ft, and stood 102ft above the College Woods. Because of the need for constant repairs, it was decided to replace it in the mid-1930s with a stone structure. The granite blocks to be used for this work lie in the foreground.

An elderly lady once told the author that she would close her eyes every time she went over the rickety wooden bridge and sometimes prayed! Not only was the old fan bridge over this valley held together with wire stays, but it was also built on a curve. In this view new granite piers have started to be built with the help of the steam crane and scaffolding.

After the granite piers were built using stone from the local quarries, steel arches were placed between them and more wood was used to form a base onto which the reinforced concrete would be poured. This would then be faced with granite blocks.

During the course of construction a temporary rail was laid for the movement of materials. Here a man is in control of a tipping truck full of hardcore.

The new viaduct is now nearing completion: the arches are built, although the scaffolding is still in position. The banks are being built up and the hardcore tipped down the sides. After completion of these tasks, it will not take long to remove the temporary line and dismantle the crane. Today the new rails and viaduct no longer carry steam engines; instead trains are pulled by diesel locomotives.

The original Penryn station, *c.* 1920. At first, the railway track formed a giant S through the station, with no straight track at all. During the 1920s a major reconstruction scheme was implemented, involving the removal of hundreds of tons of earth and the creation of straighter track. The earth was used for an embankment further up the line towards Truro. The picture also shows a Great Western wagon and goods shed on the right.

With the work of reconstruction just about completed, the new up and down tracks are in position next to the signal box, *c.* 1935. Attention is now focused on making the original track usable as a goods yard on the right. It appears that a steam train is leaving on the down line on its way to Falmouth.

The inaugural run of the Penryn to Falmouth motor bus service, 28 March 1912, by Mr Rickard of Penryn. The vehicle is a 30hp Lacre 'toast rack' (so called because the seating arrangement is like a toast rack, with individual doors each side). It has chain drive to the rear wheels, runs on solid rubber tyres and has brass electric-powered bell-shaped head- and sidelights. It has full-length running boards and curtains that drop down to cover the windows in bad weather. Starting is by handle only – hard work and potentially dangerous, as a backfire could result in a broken wrist. The bus is seen here outside the Green Bank Hotel, Falmouth.

A penny-farthing bicycle, more correctly known as an 'ordinary' bicycle. This machine is believed to have been made around 1880 and is about to take part in a carnival. The large 'penny' wheel was typically between 48 and 56 inches in diameter, the most common size being 52 inches. It had solid tyres and a simple (and probably fairly ineffective) spoon brake on the front wheel. If lighting was required, a paraffin lamp would be hung from a leather strap at the middle of the big wheel.

This group of Constantine 'Pilchard Tails' from around 1895 seem rather sombre! The adults are, from left to right, back row: John Downing, Tom Peters, Jimmy Spargo (white beard), Bert Thomas, Charlie Bishop, George Noble, -?-. Front row: Frank Toy, Charlie Bishop, -?-, William Rashleigh, Harry Tremayne, Ted Seager. The boys are unknown. The bicycles shown here are 'safety bicycles', a later development than the penny-farthing. Many Midlands car firms began by making these popular bicycles by the hundred. They cost only a few pounds and had solid tyres, leather saddles and a spoon-type brake on the front rubber tyre. The bicycle on the right has a luxury: an oil lamp.

A large horse bus named *Fairy* on the Falmouth to Helston route, waiting outside what is now a bakery in Fore Street, Constantine, *c.* 1890. The bus has fourteen people on the top and potentially another ten inside; for this load it is using three horses, and with only a block brake on steel-rimmed wheels, it would take some effort to stop at high speed. The man at the top on the roof may be Charlie Bishop, with Mr Penlerick on his right.

A pristine pony and trap taking the Tonkin family, dressed in their Sunday best, out for a ride, *c.* 1900. In the front are Charlie Tonkin and his wife and sitting behind them is their daughter-in-law.

Fred Chegwidden from Penryn, the man who took over the printing business from John Gill when he retired, sits in his 1910 15½hp Darracq in June 1918. The car was registered AF866 and once belonged to William Easom, a Penryn motor dealer. Motor car technology has developed a surprising amount between the De Dion Bouton (next page) and this, in the space of only six years. The horse-power has doubled, four cylinders and pneumatic tyres are the norm and most cars are fitted with a windscreen.

Although it was photographed outside the area covered by this book, at the Norway Inn, this 1904 8hp De Dion Bouton car belonged to Dr Austin Bearne from Penryn, who had a practice in Broad Street. He is seen standing in the centre of the picture with his wife and children. The driver is Mr Rapson and with him on the car is the motor dealer Mr Eddy. The man in the sidecar on the left is Mr Dawe, who was a fruit and vegetable merchant. This car, AF156, was one of the first to appear in Penryn and caused a lot of excitement when it was delivered. It has early pneumatic balloon tyres, brakes only on the back wheels (the brake handle is outside the car on the driver's right, with the gear stick), a pair of brass Lucas 'King of the Road' lamps, and no hood or weather protection. Although designed to carry four people, it has only a single-cylinder engine, with a top speed of 25mph (downhill!) and fuel consumption of around 25mpg. Note the impressive 'boa constrictor' horn below the lamp. The author owns a 1903 version.

The Lemon Arms public house (right), at Burnthouse, on the main road between Treluswell and Ponsanooth, c. 1910. The building still stands but it is no longer an inn. The proprietor at this time was J.T. Hellings. To the left of the alehouse is a blacksmith's shop owned by William Goodman, which again is no longer used as such.

This 'Jersey Car' belonging to bowler-hatted Mr Martin looks fully loaded at Ponsanooth, c. 1910. This could be a day's outing from the Methodist chapel. Two pairs of strong horses were needed for the load, and no doubt called for some expert handling. It must have been a wonderful sight at speed! The two lamps were probably lit only by candles.

Edward Timmins, the landlord of the Stag Hunt inn at Ponsanooth in 1894. In the donkey cart outside the pub are his wife and son and Albena Tirell, who worked for them. They appear to be dressed in their Sunday best. Edward retired from running the pub seventeen years later, in 1911.

This 1906 Maudslay belonging to Major Horsford of Bosvathick, Constantine, came to rather a nasty end at Roskrow, Penryn, in 1913. According to contemporary accounts, the brakes failed and he hit the hedge. The car has wooden wheels running on balloon tyres, brass bell-shaped headlights and a round honeycomb radiator (this was a distinguishing feature of Maudslays).

A 1913 38hp Lacre charabanc of the Penryn and Falmouth Motor Company. A year later it was commandeered for the war effort and sent to France where the original owner found himself driving it in uniform. Although still on solid rubber tyres, the bus does have electric head- and sidelights and an opening windscreen to aid ventilation. The man on the left is called Matthews. Note the double steps at the side to aid access to the bus.

A 40hp Napier charabanc registered AF1258. It was bought new in 1914 by early bus pioneer T.G. Rickard for the Falmouth route. It has a fold-away hood, paraffin sidelights and gas headlights, and is seen here fully loaded on an outing.

Parked on Falmouth Moor, with Brays Temperance Hotel and the Wesleyan chapel in the background, this 38hp 28-seater Sauer toast-rack bus was purchased new in November 1919 by T.J. Rapson of Penryn. He ran it regularly between Penryn and Falmouth. This charabanc had real leather seats and was painted dark blue. The registration number, AF2378, was later transferred to a Dennis. The proud gentleman on the right is Mr Rapson.

Cox & Son's 'Royal Standard' paraffin wagon outside their stores and office, *c.* 1920. The tank held around 300 gallons. A hoarding in the background is advertising the now defunct *Western Daily Mercury*. The chimney stack is Need's paper mill, with a Hudson Soap sign beneath it. The two-horse wagon would stay away on the road for days at a time, until all the oil had been sold. They sold the paraffin to farms and large houses in the district. From the two-gallon cans on the side of the cart, it appears that they sold petrol as well. The building on the left, the Anchor Hotel, has since been demolished, along with the other buildings in Quay Hill.

This American Reo bus chassis had coachwork built by W. Mumford of Plymouth especially for the Pelere Motor Company's Mylor to Falmouth route in the mid-1920s. The little notice in the window says 'Another Mumford Body'. CO9766 is a Plymouth registration number and the bus was owned by Willy George.

Carnival time in the late 1920s. A Treluswell Brewery lorry – with the slogan 'Beer is Best' – is decorated with flowers. Rex Collins is in the driver's seat, and Edward and Mary Collins are standing in front. The main part of the banner on the lorry reads: 'Beer is best. Try Treluswell Brewery at the Cornish Arms, Par, and Western Inn, St Austell.'

Penryn swing bridge in the mid-1920s. The sign 'Drive Slowly' was necessary because the bridge was not wide enough; this was the reason for altering it in the 1930s. It would appear that demolition has started on Freeman and McLeod's works on the left. The stationary car on the right looks like a Daimler.

West Street, Penryn, in the mid-1920s. A group of people have gathered to see the aftermath of a bus collision, leaving the two vehicles interocked and blocking the road. This is one good reason why West Street has since been made one-way! The damage to the buses was so severe that the passengers had to alight through the emergency doors.

Charlie Collins' float in the 1925 Penryn Carnival. Mr Collins is holding the pony's head after winning the first prize for his display. The seventeen year old on the right is Willie Tregonning. Charlie Collins had a milk round in Penryn in the days when milk was brought to the door in copper churns and measured into householders' own jugs. Willie Tregonning later became a market gardener and specialized in chrysanthemums.

This Manaccan horse bus has stopped at the Ferry Boat Inn at Helford after crossing the Helford river in around 1900. The driver is believed to be Mr Richards. Looking at the size of the bus, it would not carry many fare-paying passengers.

George Collins with Joey, his faithful little pony, at Hill Head where he lived, *c.* 1930. The ice cream cart was made by Tallacks the coach builders in Glasney Road in the late 1920s and was kept at Saffron Court, where the pony was also stabled. Mr Collins, his wife Gladys and his sister Betty made the ice cream in the early hours of the morning, and George then sold it at Falmouth sea front using ice from the Falmouth ice works. Anything not sold was destroyed (there were no freezers in those days). During the winter he sold fruit and vegetables. He lost his leg in an accident on his way to school in Commercial Road at seven years of age.

An outing for employees of the Penryn branch of the Cornwall Electric Power Company to Bude and Clovelly in 1948. The buses belonged to the Penryn and Falmouth Bus Company. Among those present are Mr and Mrs Jack Share, Florrie McDonald, Pam Kinsman, Mr and Mrs Chas Phillips (manager), Doris Coad, Walkie Pellow, Ginger Jones, Willie Medlyn and Bert Wright.

Another in the Pelere Motors' fleet of coaches, this Leyland Cub is on an outing in the early 1950s, at Station Hill, Redruth. The beautiful granite building in the background behind the large mail van is the Mining Exchange at Alma Place, built in 'mock Gothic style' at a cost of £500 in 1880. Upon opening, the mining business was moved from Tabbs Hotel with 109 shareholders. The lamp-post was erected in 1902 when electricity came to the town. Neither the advertising boards nor the *News Chronicle* exist any longer, but Persil is still a familiar brand. A pavement has since been constructed to protect pedestrians.

A Pelere bus is turning left out of the Moor, Falmouth, in the mid-1950s. Just off the picture on the left is the Odeon cinema, which has since given way to a Tesco supermarket, and on the right is a Barrett's shoe shop. The bus is heading towards the Prince of Wales Pier at the end of the street.

A small Dennis Ace lorry in Commercial Road, Penryn, in 1952. It has drop-sides for ease of loading and was a very versatile vehicle. This particular lorry passed through several hands, including a fruiterer and a builders' merchant.

A Leyland Tiger bus belonging to Pelere Motors, outside the company's garage in Commercial Road in 1952. The company was formed in the 1920s by the George family who lived at Pelere Farm. George was an apprentice to Collins and Williams at Ponsharden where he became a motor mechanic. There were two younger brothers, Freddie and Willie and also a sister Doris. Each of the three brothers had a bus: a thirty-seater Guy charabanc, an American Chevrolet and a twenty-seater Reo (see p. 67).

A Western National bus on Penryn Bridge in 1951. The advertisement on the roof is for Brockways, a Penzance shoe shop. The next destination for Route 45 is Carclew, an estate that once belonged to Sir William Lemon, who also owned most of Mylor village.

A Bedford utility coach owned by Mack Rickard of the Penryn and Falmouth Company, seen in 1954 on the Moor at Falmouth, outside the Town Hall. A service ran between the two towns every fifteen minutes, a distance of two miles, normally taking ten minutes for its journey. The last bus in the evening left for Penryn shortly after the National Anthem was played at the picture houses (there was one just around the corner from this view). One of the drivers, Dickie Kneebone, used to say that if the bus was full, customers should walk out to the end of Webber Street (behind the bus to the right in the picture) and wait for him there. Having safely passed the policeman at the entrance to the Prince of Wales Pier, he would then be able to pick up extra passengers who would stand all the way to Penryn.

Relaxing in the back seat of this chauffeur driven Austin convertible is Penryn's Carnival King, 'Coocher Bill', wearing his crown. The car itself is a splendid example of British workmanship, sporting a Cornish registration number, and is seen here in around 1947.

This little pony and trap would deliver locally the goods bought from Cox and Sons. It is seen here outside their offices in Quay Hill, Penryn around 1920. They were plumbing, water and sanitary engineers and copper smiths and began trading in the 1890s. The family business closed in 1967.

Four
Shipping and Works

Looking from Green Bank across the inner harbour and the start of the Penryn River towards Flushing, c. 1890. The sea walls and quays here were originally built around 1660 by Dutch engineers in the employment of Francis Trefusis. These knowledgeable Dutchmen were specialists in this type of sea defence and supervised the work carried out by local labour, using stone from the quarries in the area. Berthed on the far bank is a twin-masted coal boat.

A view over the river from near Penryn cemetery, *c*. 1890. Centuries ago chains were placed across the river to stop raiding French and Spanish pirates from plundering the town. The river is now badly silted up and only a few small vessels come up to the quays. In the left background is the lovely village of Flushing.

A view in more or less the opposite direction, from Flushing to Penryn, in 1890. The sea defence walls and quays were built so strong and need so little maintenance that they are still used and are substantially the same today as when they were built some 400 years ago.

Penryn's steel swing bridge in 1908, the year it was opened. It took the place of another wrought-iron bridge that was erected in 1828. The notice on the right gives the conditions of use of the bridge issued by Cornwall County Council.

Exchequer Quay, Penryn, 1908. This twin-masted little ship seems to have just docked, judging by the crowd and the delivery cart alongside. In those days cargoes could have been anything from live animals from Spain, which were made to swim ashore, to fruit from the Azores, as well as timber, wine, cloth, fish, tobacco etc. The building on the left is a cattle lair, where beasts were kept on the way to market. It was demolished in 1930.

The new Swing Bridge at Penryn, *c*. 1910. The people are perhaps watching the photographer setting up his tripod. This swing bridge turned through ninety degrees to enable little ships to pass through to the quays and works at Budock Creek. It was 45ft long but only 12ft wide, and weighed 50 tons. The roadway on the bridge was made of hardwood set in asphalt on steel.

The Greenbank to Flushing ferry, *c*. 1910. At this time the fare each way was only a halfpenny. The ferryman (with a flat cap, holding the oar) is believed to be Mr Tonkin and the young man holding on to the mast is John Goldsworthy. Tenpence would have been earned from one trip with twenty people aboard. With a strong pair of arms and a strong boat it did not take long to journey between the two quays – certainly it would have been quicker than trudging through the unlit lanes and streets of Penryn in those days, unless you were lucky enough to own wheeled transport.

Flushing ferrymen at work. The author can remember hailing the ferryman at Greenbank and hearing only the sound of the oars and rowlocks. The fare was sixpence and the journey was followed by a short walk into Penryn.

This rather unusual picture is taken through the mooring ropes and chains of a ship moored alongside Exchequer Quay in around 1912. This is the new bridge that took the place of the old wrought-iron swing bridge that was built in 1828 over Budock creek for the Helston Turnpike Trust. It was built by the Hayle and Perrin Foundries and was connected with the development of Commercial Road. It was vital for the increase in traffic that had previously crossed at the bottom of St Thomas Street.

Penryn River from the Green.

A calm view of the Penryn River from The Green at high tide in around 1913. The near rooftops are of Cox & Sons, the oil and petrol importers, and beyond is the Exchequer Quay, with a little ship moored alongside. On the right in the background is the granite works of John Freeman & Sons Ltd, with their overhead steam crane. There is also a little two-masted ketch at the quay.

The Town Quay, c. 1915. Alongside is a motor vessel with a 'Woodbine funnel', using its own derricks (instead of the hand crane at the end of the Quay) to unload into the carts what could be a cargo of coal sent from South Wales. There were a number of coal merchants in Penryn at that time. These ships could only reach the quay at high tide and would rest on the deep mud at low tide.

A 1920s photograph of the swing bridge open at full tide to allow the Coast Lines steam barge *Pennar* to moor alongside a wharf in the inner basin of the Glasney or Budock Creek. This has been one of the main landing places in Penryn for centuries. In the middle background near to the three men there is the jib of a crane that belonged to Freeman's granite yard and on the left is the mast of a little ship moored alongside Exchequer Quay.

The old road surface had become very badly damaged over the years because of the constant travelling back and forth of Freeman's Fowler steam traction engines, three of which were called *Alpha*, *Beta* and *Zeta*, and later the heavy lorries full of granite stone going to the Freemans yard. In 1928 the firm of A.J. Steer & Co. were given the contract to resurface the road. Using 'Ferro-crete' concrete and BRC reinforcement, the road surface was raised by 3ft to repair the damage and to reduce the risk of flooding. The total cost was under £3,000 and the work was supervised by the Borough Surveyor, J.N. Harris. Here the workmen are laying the concrete over the reinforcements, near a motor engineer's workshop.

For centuries, Commercial Road was only a footpath alongside St Gluvias' Creek. behind the long gardens of the houses of the main street. These gardens were rented out to market gardeners who sold their produce to the townspeople and also supplied shops. Quays were built as trade expanded in the early nineteenth century, and at the end of the gardens a road was developed. By the mid-1920s transport had increased to such a degree that it became necessary to widen the road, which meant demolishing the whole of the side furthest from the water. In this view from 1934, Mead's paper mill is being demolished and the waterwheel is very prominent.

The restricted width of the old swing bridge caused a dangerous bottleneck which was unsuitable for modern traffic. It was noted in August 1929 that 3,220 vehicles with a total weight of 5,500 tons had passed over the bridge. By the same month in 1935 traffic had doubled and the total weight was 10,800 tons. The County Council was authorized to build a fixed bridge with a width of 33ft and to widen the road to 60ft for a distance of half a mile at each end. The Falmouth side was the first to be modified, with the road being widened in 1931. The total cost of this phase was £16,000. This photograph shows the completed new fixed bridge in around 1936, with the Anchor Hotel behind Cox & Son's offices and showrooms.

THE BRIDGE, PENRYN

Owing to a financial crisis in 1931 work on the new bridge was postponed, but in 1934 the construction started again, and the approach road was begun on the Commercial Road side. It cost £34,000 to demolish the toll house, the old Custom House, Mead's paper mill and other buildings, while keeping the bridge open for traffic. This left approximately £39,000 to complete the new bridge. It was necessary to excavate 20ft through the river mud to obtain suitable rock foundations. Steel sheet piles were driven around the outer line of the new piers, excavated and filled with concrete. The old bridge was left in position until the construction of the new piers with beam and slab decking over them was completed each side of it. The existing swing bridge was removed and beam and slab decking replaced it. The whole of the new construction was then faced with granite. A.E. Farr were the contractors under the County Surveyor, E.H. Collcutt. Mr Hore-Belisha, Minister of Transport, opened it on 14 February 1936. Penryn's Mayor Tom Greenwood and councillors were present. This picture shows the completed bridge from the Glasney and Budock side; Exchequer Quay is the other side. As the bridge was fixed, the little vessels were no longer able to unload in the inner basin and everything was then transported by land to where they used to go. My mother told me I was the first to cross the bridge; she pushed me over in a pram at the age of nine months!

The opposite end of Commercial Road from the bridge, c. 1946. On the right is T.H. Nicholls' garage, Austin and Rover dealers and repair specialists. It is believed that the garage had previously been run by the Richards brothers and Rundles. Off to the right are St Gluvias church. Mylor and Flushing, while straight on leads to The Praze and the Cross Keys pub. To the left of the wagon in the distance is the Globe pub and to the right the building with double doors is Jan Harvey's garage, from which he ran a bus service to Falmouth in the 1950s. It was previously used by the Enys family to house their carriages when they attended St Gluvias' church at the end of the nineteenth century.

Fishing Boats, River Fal, Falmouth

Do not believe everything you read! This is not the river Fal – it is the Penryn River in August 1939. It is doubtful that any of the boats were actually used for fishing. The nearest vessel is a topsail schooner. The name on the roof of the shed on the right locates the image: it is Posnharden, a little ship repair yard with a dry dock, with Boyer Cellars in the background. Around the river to the right are Greenbank and Falmouth.

Man-e-Moors, or 'Muddy beach' as it is known locally, on the waterfront near the Church Walk. At the time of this photograph, someone walking towards St Gluvias church could well have passed the last tin smelting works in Cornwall, Sara's foundry and Dawes' fruit and vegetable warehouse. To the left is Church Walk, in the background are Harvey's buildings and to the right is the back of Commercial Road, including the rounded roof of J.C. Annear's builders' merchants. The author remembers going with friends in the 1940s to dig ragworms from the beach. We would club together to get the threepence for the return fare to Falmouth, where we would sell the ragworms to a fisherman for two shillings.

Flushing quay and war memorial, *c*. 1950, with Falmouth on the far side. It was to this quay that the first powered ferry came from Falmouth in 1870. It ran from Market Strand, Falmouth, every 10 minutes, costing ½d single and 1d return. The screw steamboat *Trefusis* was 30ft long, 8ft wide and had a draught of 3ft, and its 7hp engine was built by Messrs Sara of Penryn. The boat made a trial run between Penryn and Boyers Cellars, a distance of 2 miles, on 22 April 1870.

The *Cutty Sark* moored off Flushing, before 1938. This famous China tea clipper was built in Scotland in 1869. When fully rigged, it carried 32,000 sq. ft of sail and even when fully laden it was capable of 17 knots. Tea delivered via the Cape of Good Hope brought £3 per cubic foot when the ship was under the command of Captain George Moodie. The *Cutty Sark* had six more captains after Moody, one of whom 'walked over the side' (i.e. committed suicide). She also carried cargoes of scrap iron, coal and wool, and was the first to take a cargo of Indian tea to Australia. After the advent of steam ships and the opening of the Suez Canal, it became harder to find a cargo and the ship was sold to the Portuguese, who renamed her *Ferreira* and re-rigged as a barquentine. No longer able to earn her living, she was sold back to Captain Down, who restored her to her former glory. His widow later presented her to the Thames Nautical Training College. In 1938 and a Cutty Sark Preservation Society was formed in 1952. She remains at London to this day.

Another view of the *Cutty Sark* at anchor off Flushing. She was the last of the tea clippers, a worthy example of the glorious days of sail.

High tide at the inner dock, or Budock Creek, at Penryn, upstream of the swing bridge. The ship on the right is moored alongside the bone and manure factory. To the left is the tall smoking chimney of Fox Stanton, the timber importers. Planks of wood can clearly be seen under shelter in the distance.

The pier at Trebah beach in 1944, when Allied landings were being planned for France. Embarkation points had to be made ready and Trebah beach was chosen as one of them. To facilitate the embarkation, this pier of steel and wood was constructed, stretching out into the Helford river and changing the view along the waterfront. The hand rails, fenders and depth markers were made by Curtis & Son, Penryn. The pier was finally demolished in the early 1950s.

A coal vessel is unloading its cargo into horse-drawn carts on Durgan beach in 1909. Note the washing hung out to dry on the bushes. The coastline scenery has changed dramatically through the action of the sea at this point; it has been estimated that approximately 50 yards of cliff erosion has occurred in the last ninety years.

In this scene of 1909 are three generations of the Tonkin family, seen here at Scots Quay. The lady in the background is Mrs Tonkin Snr watching her daughter-in-law with her young grand-daughter paddling. The two ladies are dressed alike in their Edwardian skirts, blouses and straw hats. From this Quay Mr Scott exported granite, building the approach road and quay himself in 1832.

A workman with a trolley laden with recently manufactured rope at Stephens rope works at Ashfield, at the turn of the twentieth century. A young lady was killed here after he shawl became caught in some machinery. Her father, a Penryn naval pensioner, settled out of court and the family received £150 in compensation.

Freeman's stonemasons at the yard alongside the Penryn River, c. 1900. John Freeman (born 1800) and his brother first brought granite quarrying and working into prominence in this area. They first leased land on this site in 1848 and extended it by creating a quay wall of granite and in-filling behind it. By 1868 the granite works covered some three acres. All the workers are wearing cloth caps, while the supervisor at the bottom right has a hard hat.

A few years after the Freemans started their business, several quarries in the area were leased to them. Rather than work the quarries themselves, they purchased the granite from 'gangers' who employed their own men on piecework to blast out the stone and cut it to the required size. This group of stone masons from around 1910 may come from any one of a number of quarries in the Constantine area, possibly Maen Quarry. Some have small and some larger hammers, but the reason for the dogs is unknown.

John Freeman chose Penryn for the site of his works, because of the availability of large quantities of excellent granite on the surface or just beneath in the surrounding area, and because it could easily be shipped from the port of Penryn. Rough stone would be delivered to the works from the outlying quarries where it was passed to a trained mason to chisel into shape. Some contracts required perfection: for instance, in 1930, the company undertook an Admiralty contract for the Singapore Naval Base, which required water-tight faces. This meant that the granite stone had to be rubbed and polished to the required dimensions with an acceptable error of only one thousandth of an inch. The masons shown here are completing the dressing of some granite blocks, with the aid of an overhead crane.

William George Freeman (1827-1911), the son of John Freeman, came to Penryn in 1861 and was chairman of the company until his death in May 1911 at the age of eighty-four. He had headed the firm for thirty-seven years. He was greatly respected, and even though his death coincided with a serious labour dispute, several workers nevertheless attended his funeral at Falmouth, some acting as bearers.

A typical quarry at work, believed to be at Mabe, blasting out stone to feed Freeman's granite yard at Penryn. The picture shows a top-hatted foreman or perhaps ganger among his workmen. A stepped upright of a jib crane helps to move the huge blocks of stone. Relations between management and the employees were good at Freeman's. John Freeman had a reputation with his workmen for being a fair man. As a result of his popularity, his retirement in 1872 was marked in rather an unusual way. The whole of the firm marched behind Constantine band from Penryn to Falmouth, passing along the works yard that had come to a standstill, to Wood Lane where he lived in Falmouth. A dinner was held for 600 men at the Polytechnic Hall that evening. John Freeman was presented with a silver cup by his workmen in the Penryn district, as a token of their regard for him as an employer and in gratitude for his reaction to all matters affecting their welfare.

Another stone company in Penryn was William Hosken's. The concern became a limited company in 1903 and had its works in Commercial Road. The company closed in 1910 and many of the workforce moved to Freeman's. In 1913 George McLeod, a Scot born in 1875, came to the district, having formed a partnership with the Richards brothers. They had quarries at Higher Spargo, Mabe and South Brill, Constantine, trading as Richards Brothers and McLeod. Two years later McLeod broke away and kept Higher Spargo Quarry trading under his own name. He joined Freeman's and became a director in 1931; five years later the two firms amalgamated to become John Freeman and McLeod Ltd. George McLeod died in 1958 aged eighty-three whilst still managing director. This picture shows a group of masons in their protective clothing in 1914, holding their old firm's name plate.

Below opposite: John Freeman and McLeod Ltd continued to trade under that name after their managing director died in 1958, but with the decline in trade the firm closed in 1965 after 125 years of business in Penryn. The yard closed and all the equipment was sold off. This picture shows seven of the masons that were employed before the firm's closure. The men are, from left to right, Bernard Winn, Arthur Webber, John Bosanko, Harry Welch, Ernie Webber, -?-, Billy Atfield. So ended an era: this business had brought prosperity to the town of Penryn when it was in deep depression and had provided work for hundreds of men, not only in Penryn but also in the surrounding little villages.

Transport costs were low over the short distances the granite had to be hauled. The traditional way of conveying granite to Penryn was by horse-drawn wagons, with as many as six horses pulling 12 tons at a time. Drivers of the wagons were so confident of their horses that in 1846 it was common to see several strings of horses proceeding driverless in the Penryn area and, on an empty wagon behind, all the drivers sitting smoking or having their 'crouse'. It was also said that the horse teams would return home with the empty wagons while the drivers remained behind in the public houses in Penryn at all times of the night. Here is a team of four horses in line (perhaps two abreast were too wide for the lanes and also the narrow bridge they are about to pass over), heading for Freeman's yard.

Granite from the Constantine area was shipped from here at Port Navis, on a creek of the Helford River. As early as 1856 Richard Hosken advertised a quay to let where he had been trading in granite for many years. Ships of over 120 tons were able to moor easily alongside. In 1868 Freeman's had two quays to work from. One had a mason's yard with storage space and a huge travelling crane. This yard and the crane can be seen in the background of this this idyllic scene, photographed in around 1890.

Falmouth Model Laundry Ltd had its works at College Hill, Penryn. Mr Jeal was the manager. Here is the workforce of women and girls in 1930, wearing their protective clothing, with what could be a Morris Commercial van in the background. From left to right, back row: D. Griffiths, Flossie ?, S. Coombes, K. Thomas, L. Kneebone, K. Bastian, N. Toy, P. Martin, -?-, Gwennie ?, -?-. Middle row: Mrs Fuller (charge hand), M. Treleaven, Mrs Martin, Florrie ?, S. Martin, S. Norris, K. Greenwood, V. Gilbert, H. Medlin, Elsie ?, -?-. Front row: Lizzie Charman, Olive Timmins, ? Dunstan, Beattie Walker, -?-, E. Jago, Florrie Warn, ? Jenkin, ? Warn, Olive Chinn, ? Coombes.

Lower down the creek Freeman's had another quay where some Constantine granite was still being shipped to the Penryn works until the mid 1920s. The quays were well built with dressed granite blocks. Seen here is a typical example of a twin-masted sailing ship that took granite from this creek in around 1900. With the tide falling, the two men are struggling to get their rowing boat ashore.

The carpenter's shop at Treverva, c. 1900. The young man on the left is Mr Berryman. The shop was situated nearly opposite the forge, near a horseshoe-shaped lane called 'Teapot Alley' which leads round the back of the village. The cottages of the workers at the granite quarry used to stand here before being condemned and demolished in the 1930s. The village is well known these days for its renowned male voice choir, formed many years ago.

Treluswell Brewery, one mile from Penryn on the Redruth Road, was owned by W. Crang Wicket & Co. until the end of 1898, when it was sold to Sidney Hatch. Seen here is John Williams at twenty years of age with an account book in 1897. In 1913, at the age of thirty-six, he became works manager after starting as an office boy. In 1915 the brewery employed eight or ten people, and the lorry driver received £2 15s wages. Under Wickett's ownership they also brewed 'Ye Old Cornish Ginger Beer' as well as their tasty steam beer.

One of Treluswell Brewery's brewers tops up a barrel of beer, *c.* 1897. At this time the company employed two brewers, named Thackery and Hart. Bundles of hops came from Kent by train and were delivered by lorry to the brewery. The brewery used water from the stream that flowed through the premises. The beer was delivered by dray to the Three Tuns in West Street, Penryn, the Stag Hunt at Ponsanooth and other public houses in the district. The man standing on the right looks like a cooper, given the tool he is holding. Miss Williams the daughter of the owner, ran the brewery for twelve months before it closed in 1943. The same year the US Army acquired the brewery and buildings for ammunition storage and building sentry boxes, and they stationed armed guards outside.

Treluswell Brewery was a relative newcomer in the brewing industry around Penryn, as it did not begin until around 1860. In 1830 there were three breweries in the area, Andrew and Wade, Dunsford & Co. and John Share, as well as numerous inns, public houses and beer retailers. By 1853, these three brewers had gone and two new ones appeared: Dodd & Tresidder and John Powell. John Hart also had a brewery at the Stag Hunt at Ponsanooth. This picture from around 1880 shows five Penryn brewery workers. The man on the left appears to be the 'gaffer', with the watch and chain; perhaps the foreman is on the right. The man with the large shovel must have been the hops man. The names of the men and the location of the brewery are unknown.

Treverva is a small village built on the side of an old ridgeway, used by travellers between the market town of Helston and the more important granite town of Penryn. The road was used to transport the stone hauled from the local quarries firstly by horses, then traction engines and later motorized transport. This is the blacksmith's shop around 1894, with Alfred Peters standing outside. The smithy was the focal point of the village, where many travellers' horses were shod. The large sculpted granite stones around the walls of this smithy can still be seen scattered about the village.

Magdalen tin mine, seen here around 1925, is believed to be the only mine that had a woman in charge, and was situated below the Ponsanooth Viaduct. The mine was mentioned as early as the sixteenth century and was worked intermittently. It re-opened for the last time just after the end of the First World War. A new shaft was sunk here in 1924 and went below the excavations and diggings of the old miners 150 years before them. In the background can be seen the old wooden fan railway bridge, designed and erected by Brunel, which was replaced with a concrete and granite one in 1930/31.

Magdalen mine, Ponsanooth, c. 1925. During their excavations in 1924 the miners found ancient pumping gear, pipes and ladders in good condition. The problem of separating the ore was overcome when a magnetic separator was invented. This led to a fall in the price of tin, which brought about the mine's closure in 1930. With the help of belted machinery, ore was conveyed to the 'stamps' at the top of the picture. No copper was mined, but there were thin veins of tin, easily mistaken for the white iron found at another level.

100

Five

Schools

Throughout the centuries Penryn has had a number of places of learning since Glasney College was founded in 1265. Glasney became a victim of Henry VIII in the mid-sixteenth century. Queen Elizabeth I endowed a grammar school with £6 18s a year, with the proviso that three boys be taught free of charge, but this school was closed by 1839. A Methodist school was opened in Chapel Lane in 1813, later to become Penryn's primary school. In 1837 a purpose-built school was built in Commercial Road, affiliated to the Church of England, to be known as the National School. Mr Barwis opened a private school at Bell Vue a few years later, near to Enys estate. Alongside the Methodist school a much larger school was built in 1848; the two then combined and became known as the Council School. There were other learning establishments besides the two main schools, including that run by the Misses Hill at 41 Broad Street, seen here around 1910. The proprietors were two sisters; Ethel is seen here an the left. Amongst the pupils are Pearl and Eva Dale, Ruby Ferris, Alberta Toms, Jimmy and Kathleen George and Rosemary James. It would seem that the school catered for pupils of all ages from five to fifteen. When a much larger school opened, both the Council and National Schools closed. The new school was later awarded College status.

John Thomas, the first headmaster of the penny school at Ponsanooth, *c.* 1875. He was also the parish clerk and village constable, in that capacity he once took a handcuffed prisoner on foot all the way to Bodmin jail while he rode on horseback. He died in 1883 and his wife died aged ninety-seven in 1901.

Mawnan School, 1920. The school, situated at the centre of the village, opened in 1833 and closed in 1972 when a new school was built at the top of Grove Hill. The headmaster, on the right, was 'Boss' Harvey. Those pictured include: S. Treneer, T. Hocking, T. Peters, J. Hall, W. Johns, J. Orchard, E. Jenkin, E, Medlin, M. Cutter, L. Tresise, E. Tallack, A. Benney, J. Eddy, N. Pascoe, C. Medlin, J. Lawry, M. Tresise, A. Thomas. M. Sanderson, D. Benney, B. Hall, J. Johns, O. Hendy, C. Day, J. Jenkin, H. Tremaine, J. Hodge, A. Webster, R. Thomas, C. Hurst, F. Eddy.

Penryn Wesleyan School, Group 3, c. 1900. The slate on which the group's details are written is typical of the writing materials of the time, before pen and paper were commonly used in school. This establishment later became the Council School. From left to right, back row: Miss Chewidden, J. Reed, ? Toms, G. Smith, -?-, C. Richards, -?-, M. Skinner, M. Cester. Third row: G. Prello, W. Wallace, A. Richards, R. Gilbert, J. Bennetts, W. Young, R. Toy, -?-, -?-. Second row: C. Medlyn, L. Travers. F. Freeman, M. McCall, B. Walker, A. Bullen, P. Bullen, L. Rundle, I. Harris, G. Pinch, G. Williams, A. Henwood. Front row: N. Esom, A. Francis, H. Moore (with slate), W. Kneebone, C. Bath.

Penryn Council Infants' School, 1911. From left to right, back row: Dick Paul, Chappie Binney, Jack Penver, Denzil Tallack, ? Hocking, Jim Jones, Jack Chubb, Norman Hearn, John Spargo, Leonard Smith, teacher (unknown). Middle row: Florrie Kneebone, Hettie Ferris, Meba Binney, Dolly Harris, Mabel Rapson, Annie Rowe, Doris Blight, Murial Spargo, Blanche Harris, Lily Beard. Front row: Vivian Furneaux, Clarence Keast, Victor Andrew, Harold Wood, ? Harris, Gertrude Retchford, Will Harris, Cecil Wills, Edgar Opie, John Osborne.

Constantine Boys' School, 1923. From left to right, back row: H. Winn, R. Toy, C. Bowden, K. Bishop, L. Vague, G. Gendle, teacher Mr Dunn, H. Roberts, J. Cocking, N. Williams, G. Rowe, -?-. Front row: B. Symonds, M. Dunstan, R. Combellack, Ronnie Matthews, H. Winn, E. Rowe, J. Hocking, J. Symons, B. Truscott.

Penryn Council School, 1925/26. The teacher on the left is Miss George. From left to right, back row: C. Gilbert, D. Curgenvan, G. Dunstan, H. Hoskin, V. Grace, G. Bowers, V. Tripp, J. Martin. Third row: W. Ball, B. Pellow, P. Ackenhead, I. Martin, S. Gilbert, M. Newman, H. Best, D. Webber, K. Newman. First row: B. Morris, M. Warne, D. Pearce, K. Woods, J. Annear, V. Martin, E. Pomeroy, J. Rogers. Bottom row: R. Buckingham, D. Martin, C. Kendall, S. Honey, J. Sara, V. Warmington (the author's uncle).

Mabe School, 1943. The teacher was Mr Putts. From left to right, back row: I. Young, N. Rolling, -?-, D. Pascoe. D. Pellow, ? Evans, B. Hoskin, ? Wilson, P. Rogers, R. Doney. Middle row: R. Lovers, W. Farman. Front row: V. Richards, M. Richards, O. Burley, A. Hosken, P. Tremain, P. Rechford.

Penryn Council School, 1946/47. From left to right, back row: Derek Bennett, Melville Berry, Lyman Rickard, Billy Reed, Cyril Pellow, Leslie May, Cecil Webb, Douglas Pellow, Mr Davison (teacher). Middle row: Brian Hosking, Ivor Rundle, Christine Able, Heather Richards, Margaret Smith, Ian Butland, Noel Magor. Bottom row: June Fuller, Eunice Bolitho, Elizabeth Head, Marjorie Lawry, Jean Palarm, Lily Bradley, Edwina Odgers, Maureen Burns.

Penryn National School, 1948. From left to right, back row: Nancy Blackler, Jean Sleeman, Betty Lane, Molly Newman, Gloria Binny, Yvonne Tregonning. Middle row: Tony Able, Tony Toy, Frank Berriman, Claude Churcher, Geoffrey Ferris, Miss Toomy (teacher). Front row: Pamela Hocking, Betty Kerslake, Mary Arthur, Tommy Gill (headmaster), Joy Phillips, Cynthia Mallet, Christine Maddison.

National School, Penryn, 1950/51. From left to right, back row: T. Gill (headmaster), M. Preston, B. Richards, M. Smith, R. Young, G. Sloggett, E. Bowers, D. Toy, J. Simmons, C. Bowers. Middle row: R. Minson, L. Tregoning, P. Timmins, S. Walker, S. Phillips, M. Simmons, M. Grimshaw, P. Toy, M. Morris, J. Lawry. Front row: C. Blair, V. Crocker, S. Browning, A. Tregoning, G. Vincent, Miss Davies, R. Newman, M. Treglown, V. Toy, L. Collison, B. Mallett.

Six

Sport

Regarded as one of the earliest rugby clubs in Cornwall, Penryn RFC was formed in 1872 and played their home matches at Green Lane. When Marshall Thomas was captain they won the Cornish Championship (losing one match only, to Hayle) in 1877. By 1888 the club was forced to disband because many of the miners who formed the majority of the team had emigrated. William Halls returned after five years away and reformed the club. Halls played at full back not only for Penryn but for the county team as well. A weekly magazine, *Answers*, offered £5 to anyone in the UK who kicked a rugby ball the furthest. Billy Halls entered and won with a kick of nearly 80 yards (and that with a heavy leather ball, which was even heavier when wet; how far would it have gone using a modern ball?). He would certainly have gone for three points on his own twenty-two line. This picture shows Penryn RFC in 1884. From left to right, back row: J. Reynolds, A. Pinche, W. Halls, A. Newcombe, N. Thomas. Middle row: J. Bunny, D. Newcombe, A. Vincent, J. Timmins, T. Vincent, P. Sara, P. Dadson. Front row: W. Pinch, T Moore (captain), R. Martin.

The rugby club kept going through the lean years that followed, mainly thanks to the efforts of one player, George 'Mashie' Collins, who persevered and was an outstanding figure. The club produced few county players until after the First World War; only George Jago (who captained Cornwall on the wing at Bradford against Yorkshire in 1927/28) and Dr Hopper. Between the wars, G. Jago, Harry Richards and A.L. Richards won county caps. George Jago played in almost every Cornish team during the 1920s. His brothers Charles and Harry also played for Cornwall, as did their father before. This photograph shows Penryn RFC in 1934/35. From left to right, back row: J. Eddy (first aid officer), G. Pellowe (treasurer), J. Jacket, E. Lampshire, W. Trounce (secretary), W. Roberts, A. Richards, J. Thomas, C. Christophers (team secretary) J. Leggassick (committee), J. Young (committee). Middle row: J. Martin, F. Young, L. Martin, E. Jose, G. Jago, (captain), R. Rogers, H. Jago, H. Richards, J.Rickard (trainer). Front row: D. Martin, C. Pearce. D. Rogers (mascot), J. Richards, A. Binney.

Below opposite: I well remember my father, a keen Penryn supporter, taking me to watch them play in the late forties. During the 1950s, some really outstanding players played at Penryn, such as Ted Rose (who came form Lancashire), Ivan Richards, Maurice Keast, Fred Chamberlain, Ron Edney, John Cobner and a few others; these all played for the county. Ken Plummer and Roger Hosen also gained international honours more than once. Arguably the best player was Vic Roberts, who captained Cornwall, England and the British Lions at wing forward. Roberts, Hosen and Plummer were later presented with the Freedom of the Borough of Penryn. Penryn RFC is seen here in 1955/56. From left to right, back row: 'Pippy' Head, R. Rogers, R. Hosen, I. Zedmin, A. Perkins, B. Bate. Middle row: A. Ahens, D. Young, I. Richards, E. Rose, L. Roff, R. Paull, M. Keast. Front row: A. Martin, J. Cobner.

In 1946 Penryn Rugby Club, under the leadership of the secretary Nelson Barrett, bought and improved the old Parkangue playing field (with the help of the Council School boys), renaming it The Memorial Ground in memory of the club players who died in the two world wars. The new ground came into use in September 1947. Here is Penryn RFC in 1953/54. From left to right, back row: Alan Ahens, 'Pippy' Head, R. Rogers, Shaun Black, Michael Wills, Tony Parkin, Brian Bate, Cedric Martin, Raymond Paul. Middle row: Alfie Martin, Danny Young, Ted Rose, -?-, John Cobner, Les Roff, Maurice Keast. Front row: Raymond Plummer, Paul Williams.

No team is without its supporters' club and Penryn is no exception. Here can be seen the ladies during the 1951/52 season, dressed in the club's colours (at that time red and black) and sporting county and international caps won by the players of the club. The ladies also had great fun playing the men at Glasney playing field during Carnival week. From left to right, back row: Mrs Penver, J. Plummer, B. Quintrell, -?-, N. Barrett. Third row: M. Pardoe, P. Martin, M. Penver, Mrs Quintrell, K. Webber, Mrs Martin, D. Penver, Mrs Rowe. Second row: Mrs Webb, J. Roff, -?-, S. Martin (with ball), I. Plummer, R. Bolitho, -?-. Front row: F. Plummer, P. Penver, J. Keast.

In the early 1930s Penryn had a remarkable boxing club. Their gym was in New Street and cost 10s a week (including electricity) to rent from a builder. Harold Thomas was their trainer and promoter. Amongst the fighters were Jack Chinn, Billy Simmons and Eric Blake. The star of the club was Billy Roberts, seen here aged nineteen. He was 6ft 1in tall and weighed 13½ stone; he was by trade a motor mechanic and chauffeur. He also played first team rugby for Penryn and had a county trial. In 1934 before a packed Temperance Hall he knocked out Bill Jury from St Ives in two rounds to become the Cornish Heavyweight Champion. He went on to fight bigger men from 'up country', including sparring partners for Jack Peterson and Primo Carnera, famous heavyweights; he beat both. Everywhere he went to fight he attracted packed houses. He was at one time the number one contender for the West of England Championships. On one Saturday he played in a county rugby trial at Camborne in the afternoon, rushed home for tea and sped up to Wadebridge to fight and win a fifteen-round fight in the evening. Bill suffered just six defeats in over 100 fights. The final bell went for him when he broke a leg playing rugby.

Below opposite: Vic Roberts of Penryn Rugby Club being carried shoulder-high after returning from his first game for England, against France, in 1947. He not only went on to captain his country but was also privileged to lead the British Lions. The welcoming party has gathered at Truro station and includes Penryn's Mayor and Mayoress and members and players of the Penryn Rugby Club. Others present are: Nelson Barrett (honorary secretary), George Jago, Jack Chinn, Vic Roberts, Ron Edney, Reg Bolitho, Benny Jennings (Mayor), Mrs Jennings, Mrs Roberts.

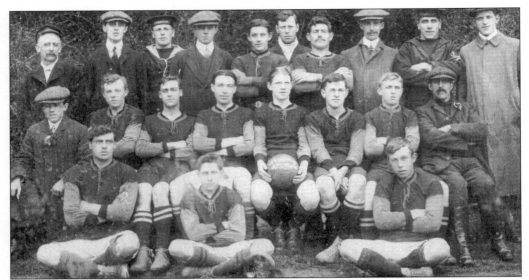

Flushing FC in 1910/11, when they were champions of Second Division Falmouth and District League. From left to right, back row: W. Nicholls (committee) G. Cleave (honorary secretary and treasurer) W. Swadling, C. Beckett, N. Pitick, A. Luke (referee), C. Thomas, C. Pover, A. Blake, P. Harding (linesman). Middle row: A. Smale, J. Pascoe (vice-captain), J. Monk, G. Ellis, H. Hallett (captain, with ball), S. Wernhard, G. Raglan, B.Gilbert. Front row: W. Laity, L. Young, W. Hurrell. In the picture there are also two sailors from the *Foudroyant*, a training ship often seen in the bay off Flushing and Falmouth, one in a summer top and lanyard and the other in winter attire. They could be members of the Flushing club, or perhaps spies for their next game! Why is the 'lucky horseshoe' upside down?

Penryn Cricket Club of 1956/57 after a prize-giving at the Anchor Hotel. The silver cup being held by the captain is believed to be for the winners of the Penryn and Falmouth Cricket League. From left to right, back row: B. Hellings, -?-, Joe Martin, John Henna, George Wills, Derek Williamson. Middle row: Alan Ruse, Clive Willey, Philip Smith, Paul Toy, John Sloggett. Fron row: Raymond Dunstan, ? Barnes.

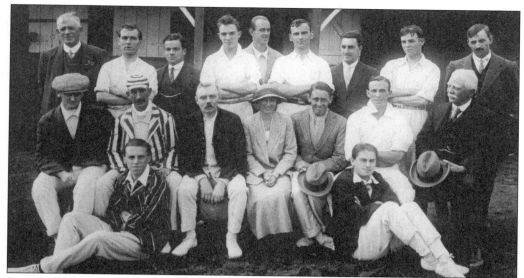

Penryn Cricket Club is believed to have played their home matches at Parkangue next to the Rugby Club and opposite the ground where St Gluvias' Cricket Club now plays. There are reports of cricket being played in Penryn towards the end of the nineteenth century, but it then seemed to fade away, to return again in the 1920s. The club was re-formed once more after the Second World War. Bernard Bishop and Alfie Kerslake later formed a break-away club at Pencoose Farm, which after a short while moved to The Glebe (near to St Gluvias' church). They now play on their own pitch at Parkangue opposite the original ground. This photograph shows the original Penryn Cricket Club in 1923. From left to right, back row: F. Faull, B. Down, C. Richards, (honorary secretary), G. Jago, L. Vivian, F. Richards, C. Pinch, L. Smith, R. Smith. Middle row: T. Treloar, D. Dempster (vice-captain) G. Fairbrother (president), Miss Blamey, Dr N. Blamey (captain), F. Smith, Dr J. Blamey. Front row: C. Bradley, H. Pearce.

Penryn Cricket Club in around 1947, when they played at Parkangue. From left to right, back row: A. Kerslake, Horace Hancock, Bert Morley, Stanley Jewell, Des Jenkin. Middle row: Barry Quintrell, Peter Cremin, Cyril Kendall, Tom Pardon, Arthur Maunder. Front row: Bernard Bishop, Buster Craig, John Henna.

Mawnan Bowls Club was formed in 1924 by Lord and Lady Rendlesham. His Lordship gave the club £150 towards the construction of a new green, which was opened in 1929 at Mawnan Smith on land given by Mrs Hodgkin. The new ground was constructed in a short time by club volunteers who were given time off by the large estates at no cost. The picture shows the Bowling Club in around 1950. From left to right: E. Eddy, -?-, J. Paget, -?-, -?-, D. Day, J. Chinn, -?-, Revd A. Gunstone, A. Pascoe, F. Rowe, W. Barbary.

Penryn Liberal Club's darts team around 1955, with their trophies and medals won during the season in the Penryn and Falmouth League. From left to right, back row: ? Thomas, Eddy Burleigh, Stanley Woodward, Rufus Toy. Front row: Bill Blackmore, John Carlyon, Bill Burleigh, Brooke Rogers, Jack Williams.

In 1830 the proprietor of the Three Tuns Inn in Pig Street was Anne Bahanna; in 1852 the landlady was Peggy Treloar but the street had been renamed West Street. There are only three public houses still open with their original names in Penryn out of the fifteen that existed in 1852. The Cornish Arms, also in Pig Street, with landlord William Allin in 1830, was later renamed the Fifteen Balls. Richard Thomas managed it in 1852. Here is the darts team from the Three Tuns Inn around 1950, when the proprietor was Mr Blake. From left to right, back row: Reg Searle, Rex Morrish, Cliff Coombes, Ivy Toy, Ockey Toy, Roy Blake Gordon Coombes. Front row: Bill Timmins, Ron Messer.

Constantine FC played at the Recreation Ground and are seen here with the huge Wheatly Cobb Shield and medals won during the 1933/34 season in the Falmouth and District League. From left to right, back row: R. Toy, Bill Symons, Albert Williams, Morley Rashleigh, George Symons, George Tramayne, Reg Hyde, G. Fletcher, Henry Sanders, Billy Rashleigh. Middle row: A. Soult, H. Mitchell, Fred Blewett, Harry Phillips, Sol Phillips, Monty Dunstan, Ewart Rowe. Front row: Cliff Bastian, Garfield Williams.

Penryn AFC, winners of the Goldman Cup and Lockhart Cup and runners-up in the Western Division of the Cornwall Junior Cup, c. 1920. From left to right, back row: S. Burns, W. Burleigh, C. Rickeard. Third row: H.B. Jennings, E. Burleigh, L. Baker, T.A. Dobson, E.J. Thomas (vice-captain), N. Rich (captain), H. Hodge, C. Cock, R. Scantlebury, I. Thomas (trainer). Second row: G. Burleigh, H.L. Vivian (honorary treasurer), L.T. Cole (chairman), C.W. Andrew (president), B.D. Down (honorary secretary), J. Andrew. Front row: B. Sewell, C. Jennings, C. Jago.

Mawnan Cricket Club celebrated its centenary in 1979. They first played on Boskensoe Downs, then in 1935 moved to their present ground at the Playing Field. Resuming after the war in 1946 they won the Western Morning News Cup, followed by the Vinter Cup in 1947. The team is seen here in around 1952. A. Christophers, R. Sara, -?-, -?-, -?-, L. Symons, H. Howard, -?-, C. Sara, J. Hodge, C. Eddy, S. Trewhella.

Seven

Fire Brigade and People

Penryn's first fire engine, c. 1760. It must be one of the oldest in the county. It was made of hardwood with a lead-lined water container and ran on four solid wood wheels with metal rims; it was drawn by two horses. By moving the side levers in a pumping action, the two single-action pumps were activated with the aid of an air vessel, enabling a smooth flow of water from the canvas hoses. It was probably filled by hand with buckets before use. No accounts survive in the borough's records as to how much was paid for the engine, but another town in Cornwall paid £41 12s for one a little while later. From the borough's accounts of 1761/62 a Thomas Pearce was paid 10s for 'oiling ye engine pipes'; a further 14s was paid to James Pellow in 1763 for 'cleaning Fire Engine Ho' (is this 'Houses' or 'Hoses'?). £1 13s 9d was spent on repairs in 1766 (it was not reported what for). John and Richard Nicholas took care of the engine from 1767 to 1774, for which they were paid the princely sum of 14s per year.

Penryn's second fire engine was bought by public subscription in 1827. It was sold in 1887 to provide more hose for the third engine. The Fire Chief had recommended the sale of both manual engines, but for sentimental reasons the town kept its 1760 fire engine. The first and third engines are in remarkably excellent condition and can be seen, together with a hand-drawn ladder cart, in the town's museum. Eighteen fire men can be seen posing in their brass helmets alongside the third fire engine in this scene from around 1915.

There was a fire in the Town Hall and Market House at Penryn in 1773 (the building now houses the town's museum). Repairs cost £1 4s 9½d and no less than £1 3s 0d was spent on liquor for those who helped to put the fire out. A further 12s was paid on 19 April 1773 for 'the care of the fire engine'. It is possible that the fire was connected with the tinners' riot in the town in February 1773. In the next year's account 15s 4d was spent on repairing the engine and a sum of £3 19s 7d was paid to James Pellow for an engine house. Thereafter, entries in the accounts seem to end, presumably because the engine had been moved out of the Town Hall to a new safer site, possibly the 1899 building at the top of St Thomas Street. The picture shows a parade of fire engines being led by Penryn's third fire engine in 1903; on the left are the Seven Stars and The Terrace.

Below opposite: The town council voted a sum of £30 towards the purchase of Penryn's third fire engine on 28 August 1887. The engine is seen here in around 1920. Fundraising was difficult but a 'Jubilee' engine was purchased from the well-known London firm of Shand Mason & Co. The engine and equipment were insured against loss by fire in November of that year. As insufficient hoses had been purchased and given that the fire station very damp, the captain of the brigade again advised the council to sell the two old fire engines and 'apply the money to new hoses'. The oldest one was kept. The lettering 'Penryn' can just be made out on the side of the engine.

The 'Jubilee' fire engine was drawn by two horses and could transport the firemen as well as the water to the scene of the fire. However, valuable time was wasted in catching the horses that were kept near to St Gluvias' church at The Glebe, which is some considerable distance from the fire station. For instance, in July 1919 when Tremough House was in danger of being burnt, the fire engine and hose and ladder cart were pulled by hand for a mile and a half because the horses could not be caught. This is Mr Finch, a member of the brigade in around 1920, sporting his long-service medals.

Damage to a house in Budock, which was razed to the ground in the late 1920s, was exacerbated by the fact that two Penryn firemen had to struggle in the dark and wet to harness the horses and bring them to the fire station. After this, Messrs Webber's lorry was used to tow the Jubilee engine until the first motorized fire engine was purchased in the early 1930s. This was Penryn's fourth recorded engine. This is one of Penryn's firemen in the late 1920s, Station Officer H. Worsdell, with his forty-five years' service medal and bars.

The first motorized fire engine used in Penryn was obtained in the early 1930s and is believed to have been a Dennis. Here is the engine with its ten firemen, as well as the hoses with a suction basket end on one.

Members of the National Fire Service, part-time officers attached to the Penryn Division as part of the war effort, seen with their engine (possibly a Dennis) in the 1940s. From left to right, on the vehicle: -?-, Ben Williams, Joe Gainey, Ken Benny, F. Coombes, Dickie Dunstan, driver B. Blank. In front: R. Bolitho, Les Jenkin, Chief Officer T. Thompson. The sign-written text 'Borough of Penryn' is clearly visible.

The closure of Penryn fire station at the top of St Thomas Street (built in 1899) was proposed in 1948 but rejected due to local opposition. The fire station was relocated to Commercial Road, near to St Gluvias Street, in 1981 but the brigade was amalgamated with the Falmouth branch in April 1996. Here is a group of Penryn firemen outside the Red Lion during a church parade. From left to right: Peter Mitchell, Sid Oliver (station officer), M. Burrley, Jim Hodges, Roy Wills, -?-, Peter Coombes, Gerald Collins (sub-officer), Peter Curgenven (leading fireman).

My grandmother in around 1916, with her son (my father) on the right and daughter Elsie. She is holding baby Verdom. There is a striking family resemblance between my father and my brother, to whom this book is dedicated.

Mr L.J.C. Peter lived on The Terrace, Penryn, and was a pupil at the Methodist School, Chapel Lane. He wrote the Lord's Prayer on an area the size of a sixpence, despite having no hands. On the right is an enlarged copy of his text.

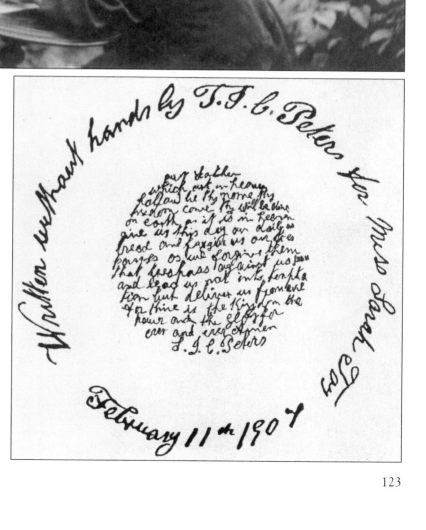

In 1907 Penryn's first fish and chip shop opened at 107 Helston Road. It was run by Dickie Paul and sold all types of fish, including small whiting known as 'toms', cod, hake and flat fish at a penny a piece. The fish came straight from Newlyn market where the auctioneer was a member of the family, at the low price of £1 per barrel. It was delivered by rail and cooked on a new coal range. The fat came from Porthleven in barrels delivered by horse and trap. There was reports that enough barrels had been washed up after a ship had been wrecked to last twelve months. Potatoes were grown in the large garden at the rear of number 107. In connection with the chip shop, there used to be a local rhyme: 'You kiss a girl from Budock and onions you will taste; You kiss a girl from Flushing and it tastes like bloater paste; You kiss a girl from Penryn and on these tempting lips You will taste the yum-yum flavour of Dickie Paul's fish and chips.' The establishment later became a wet fish shop. This picture shows John Barnicoat, Dickie Paul (with the fish), Paul and Clive Barnicoat in around 1936.

Freemasonry was first recorded in Penryn in 1782. The Masons met at the King's Arms Hotel, but ceased to meet after twenty-seven years. While that lodge was in operation another was formed, known as the Three Grand Principles, and met at the Golden Lion in 1799. It was later renamed The Red Lion (the Masonic symbols can still be seen above the entrance). It became established once again at The Kings Arms in 1863. The lodge moved to a purpose-built hall at the bottom of New Street in 1912 and has remained there ever since. The hall was erected by the Barnicoat family at a cost of £850. The Masons of the time were, from left to right, back row: E. Sara, R. Bishop, A. Roberts, E. Roach, F. Sara, H. Chubb, A. Hosking (Steward), B. Thomas, F. Harris, T. Johns, F. Barnicoat SW, B. Hosking, S. Andrew. Middle row: T. Barnicoat JD, J. Paul, H. Sara, R. Sumers, A. Baxter, R. Ashford Steward, R. Huss, P. Thomas, F. Roberts, S. Andrew. H. Chubb, E. Johns, C. Rusden SD, H. Dunstan. Front row: C. Rowe, SD, A. Geach PGD, N. Grey (Chaplain PPGSW), R. Newcombe PM PPGD, M. Truscott IPM, G. Elliot WM, R. Dunstan SW, R. Roberts JW, J. Lawrey (Treasurer), F. Chegwidden (Secretary), T. Dunstan PM, F. Jewell PM.

Falmouth Carnival Queen of 1933, Miss Hilda Tripp. For the second successive year Penryn had the honour of providing the Carnival Queen for the Falmouth and District Hospital Carnival Week, in an open competition for the whole district. Miss Tripp and her eight attendants were crowned by the retiring Queen, Miss Marjorie McColl, at the Town Quarry. Among her duties she witnessed water sports on Saturday. On Monday she drove around Castle Drive, Falmouth, where motor cycle races were held, filmed by Movietone News. She met the chief prize-winners and distributed prizes after starting races at the Recreation Ground. On Wednesday with her eight attendants she attended a fête at Gyllyngdune Gardens and in the evening distributed prizes at a whist drive. On Carnival Saturday, they were driven around in coaches and pairs. Miss Tripp, now Mrs Coad, now lives in Torquay.

John Gill, who was born at St Ive in 1811. He became an apprentice at twelve years of age with a Truro bookbinder and stayed there for seven years. In 1831 he rented a shop opposite the old King's Arms in Penryn. After borrowing money to buy a second-hand printing press in 1838, he made a profit of £200. He married a Sunday school teacher in 1835 and had seven children. 1867 saw the first edition of *The Commercial Shipping and General Advertiser*, which was later to became *The Penryn Advertiser*. Fred Chegwidden, who worked for John Gill, bought the business shortly before Gill's death in 1905 at the age of ninety-five.

Penryn schoolchildren enjoying a celebration. The occasion is probably the Coronation of Queen Elizabeth II in 1953.

Members of Penryn Borough Council outside the Town Hall in 1962/63. The marble plaque on the wall behind relates to the lighting of the the town clock's faces in 1909. From left to right, back row: Sgt L. Dobson, J.W. Armstrong, R. Gardner, W.H. Pellow, J. Young, W.C. Martin, W.P. Manning, PC C.J. Burley. Middle row: R.J. Oppy, H.W. Gravestock, J.F.C. Tregenza, L.F. Campbell, D.H.L. Thomas, D.M. Williams, M.A.L. Edwards, A.C. Dunstan, C.H.G. Probert. Front row: E.C. Gwyther, E.F. Wilde, W.G. Bestherick, Mark Tallack (Mayor), P.M. Tallack, B.N. Wilde, E.W. Medlin, W.G.H. Kingdon.

Constantine 'postie' Edwin Medlyn, seen here at Sevorgan post box around 1900.

There have been a number of colourful hawkers and street traders in Penryn over the years. This is Lizzy Shirdy, or 'Happy Lizzie' as she was known, in 1905. Her real name was Elizabeth Dunstan and she came from Stithians. The generation gap did not exist for this loveable character, who will be remembered by many older folk for her tuneful renderings to Penryn children. She would often sing this song: 'Sunday I am happy, Monday full of joy, Tuesday I've a peace of mind no evil can destroy, Wednesday and Thursday I'm walking in the light, Friday is a heaven below, so is Saturday night.' She would also enter a grocer's shop, pick up same goods and say 'I can't pay, but the Lord will repay you', and walk out. After several such occurrences, she would say, 'I am not walking out West Street, because it is too windy,' meaning she owed too much money to the shopkeepers in that part of town!